D1715196

Chasing Normal, Finding Hope

{my story of a decade with mental illness}

By Leah Nash

To the Reader

In sharing my story, I pray these words will bring comfort to those who are fearful and offer a glimmer of hope to those who are down. My heart breaks with you - all who are struggling with mental illness. These short stories illustrate snapshots of a journey plagued by my own mental illness.

Even during my most challenging times, I was surrounded by friends and family who loved me deeply; However, I still felt alone in the magnitude of my struggles. I did not know anyone with similar experiences, and I felt like a cursed outcast.

I pray this book provides a sense of camaraderie as we learn to navigate the emotions, setbacks, and struggles that mental illness places before us. Though our lives will undoubtedly take different twists and turns, be encouraged that you are not alone.

Dear One, there is hope, even in the darkest of situations. The pain that threatens to engulf is not capable of lasting forever. As a suicide survivor, I know firsthand that mental illness can uproot the world as we know it, but it does not have to end it.

If you are struggling, please always remember that regardless of how down and destitute you feel, we are absolutely ALWAYS better off with you here.

Introduction

This book is a glimpse into a life with bipolar - an account of the struggle to make sense of mental illness as it permeates every aspect of life. As is often the case, there are coexisting conditions. Bits and pieces of my other diagnoses (an eating disorder, post-traumatic stress disorder, and generalized anxiety disorder) weave their way into this story as well.

It is a journey with many ups and downs, both blessed with advances and tormented by losses. Maintaining hope remains a constant struggle but a struggle worth enduring.

Although this is a book about me, it isn't actually about ME. It is a story dedicated to all who struggle or watch a loved one struggle with mental illness.

Hold on tight. It's a bumpy ride.

Trigger warning: things get really bad before they get better.

Please don't give up on the journey described in this book because it is difficult and heartbreaking.

Mental health issues feel so different in the moment than they do looking back. Areas that seem hopeless and dark may later reveal a specific purpose. This journey has undoubtedly changed me - I would like to think for the better.

There are so many things I know now that I did not realize at the time. There are things I wish I could have said to my younger self. This is the hope I wish I could have shared.

These words are the validation that you ARE going through hell right now. These pages scream that your struggles have a purpose, it all makes sense, and there is hope. You don't have to let this overcome you.

Don't give up! Spoiler alert: Things do (in time) get better. Light indeed pierces the darkness.

This is my story of living with mental illness. After numerous ECT treatments, my memory is plagued with missing pieces, gaping holes spanning months and even years. I will tell my story as I know it - how my mind has made sense of it all. However, I must be careful: What follows isn't my experience alone. I have struggled with the decision of using our real names, not wanting to participate in the continual shaming of those who have a mental illness. Ultimately, I need to protect those around me, especially my children, whose lives would undoubtedly be affected by this public account. For this reason, names and identifying characteristics have been changed.

{contents}

{cherished childhood}

Longing for Mental Stillness
Medical Staff Fighting for My Life When I am Not
May 2010

If you had asked me five years ago, or even a year ago, if I could ever see myself attempting suicide, I would have blurted out, "Absolutely not." I had never fully experienced the depths of depression and how firm its grasp can be. I knew I'd missed some days at work. I was aware that I spent the majority of my days crying, but I've always been an optimistic, highly grateful person. But even these qualities prove insufficient to save me from the terror of depression.

I slowly crack open my eyes. Where am I? Sluggishly looking through a set of sliding glass doors, I make out nurses gathered behind a counter. I draw my gaze downward toward my body, lying weak in a hospital bed. *Crap. It didn't work.* I don't remember the sequence of events that got me here, but this certainly wasn't part of the plan; I didn't intend ever to wake up.

I reach over the railing of the bed, grabbing a plastic patient belonging bag. I methodically place it over my head while quickly pulling the drawstring.

A scream pierces the silence, "What are you doing? Get that off!" I feel the bag being yanked off my head. I'm left staring into the eyes of a frantic nurse.

I do not want to be alive. I long for nothing more than to escape the persistent psychological pain. Death feels like the only option for this soul-deep sorrow that pierces my veins.

But for now, I am forced to be alive. The medical staff has made that decision for me.

The nurse comes in a bit closer. "Do you know where you are?" I remain silent. "You're in the ICU. You took a bunch of pills and have been out for three days."

"Where are my kids?" I ask.

"Your parents have been keeping them while looking after you as much as possible."

I have no concept of the time. "Where is everyone now?" I question.

The nurse informs, "It is 5 a.m. Your parents have gone home for the night, but I'm sure they would like to know you're awake." She brings a telephone over to my bedside and helps me make the phone call.

In a slow, groggy voice, I muster up, "Hi, Mom." I hear her instantly burst into tears.

Mom sobs, "I'm so glad you're okay." There is background noise beneath the crying, the distinct sound of my mother quickly shuffling out the door rushing to come to be by my side.

When Mom arrives in the hospital room, she is still quivering. "Today is Mother's Day." she manages. "This is the best present ever - to have you alive."

I feel terrible for the pain I've inflicted. I never meant to hurt anyone else. My attempt centered on genuinely believing I'd become such a burden that everyone would be better off without me. Ending my own pain obliterated the capability of considering others' feelings and the devastating toll it would take on them.

I continue looking into Mom's face, trying to piece together the last few days. I remember a minor blip, standing in my bedroom swallowing handfuls of pills at a time, bottle, after bottle, after bottle.

Apparently, that morning I got up and took my children to school as usual and returned home to carry out a plan: writing a suicide note and gathering stockpiled medication. Mom shares that she, my emergency contact, was notified by my work that afternoon of a no-call/no-show. Aware of the severity of my depression and fearing the worst, Dad and Mom requested a police escort to the house. That is where I was found, unconscious and convulsing on the floor.

Once deemed medically (but far from psychiatrically) stable, I am transferred from the Intensive Care Unit to the Adult Unit of a neighboring psychiatric hospital.

Background

It hadn't always been this way - I haven't always had to cope with such intense feelings or contend with thoughts of suicide. Before we go forward, we need to go back to the beginning.

My mind scans back to early childhood when life seemed rather typical. I grew up in a two-parent, upper-middle-class home in the heart of the South. Dad traveled quite a bit but remained engaged when he was around, smoothly alternating from financial spreadsheets to family life. Mom was a stay-at-home parent, available for everything we needed, even showing the ultimate level of commitment–da-da-da-dum–room mom. My Brother Andrew (who is two years younger) and I shared good times climbing around our tree fort, riding bikes in the cul de sac, and flying down the slip'n slide in the summer.

We never went without; there was plenty of food on the table and gifts during the holidays. Our home was always comfortable, except for the temperature, which was directly related to Dad's penny-pinching mindset, not a dire financial shortage.

My biggest complaint was that Dad and Mom were too protective, excessively sheltering us for as long as they could. Their strong religious convictions determined their parenting styles, leaving us hiding from trick-or-treaters on Halloween and banned from typical childhood favorites like "Aladdin" and "Beauty and the Beast."

On the flip side, they never missed an opportunity to tell us kids how much we meant to them. Every day, I was reminded how very loved I was.

Despite some quirks, I think it's fair to say my Brother and I did pretty well in the nurturing department of the ongoing nature vs. nurture debate.

I like to think back to those days. What would life be like now if those innocent, happy days continued? What if mental illness never picked MY life to wreak havoc upon? However, my daydreaming doesn't last long. My fantasy world is pierced by the harsh reality that I do indeed have undeniable psychiatric struggles.

When I look back over my childhood, it is typically for a few particular reasons. I want an explanation for why I am the way I am. I am not looking to blame anyone. I am looking for understanding. What went wrong? Was it avoidable?

I seek to find answers to stop the cycle, to prevent my children from ending up in the state I'm in. I fully recognize their genetic predisposition, so I dream of insulating them in emotional bubble wrap to cover the environmental aspect. If only I could make their lives damn near perfect, maybe the mental illness fairy would pass over them. Put that wand away, far from tapping their little minds. Ridiculous, I know. But I still try. I want nothing more than happiness and regulation for them, something that will be fleeting for me.

For now, I analyze my childhood.

The Bed From Wal-Mart
April 1991

As I think of my childhood, I am taken back to my earliest, extremely goofy memories. I am four, and my Brother is two years old. We sneak into my parents' bedroom and climb under their covers. We hush each other and attempt to be as quiet as possible, which proves difficult for two giggly kiddos.

My parents magically show up and begin looking for us. "Where are the kids? We have looked everywhere and can't find them. Oh, no, we've lost our kids. This is terrible!" they exclaim.

They dramatically pretend to look under the bed, in closets, and even in dresser drawers.

The game always concludes in the same manner. My parents are "exhausted" from looking for us and decide to lie down in their bed.

"What is wrong with this bed? There are lumps." My parents swat at the bumps, which are our tiny, squirming bodies. We chuckle uncontrollably by the time we reach this phase of the game.

And then the famous last lines, "This bed is terrible. We should return it to Wal-Mart." (I'm pretty sure my parents did not purchase the bed at Wal-Mart, but that's just how this game goes.)

With those words, we pop out. "It's not the bed. It's us!" We all laugh.

This ridiculous game plays out morning after morning and will remain one of my fondest memories.

20 Years Before I - Before Anyone - Had a Clue
August 1991

There seems to be this specific line of demarcation for anyone who has suffered a drastic change in life. Before ___ happened. After ___ happened. As a little girl, I never dreamed mental illness would strike me. I played just like anyone. I laughed just like anyone. Of course, I had no idea what bipolar was, and I certainly did not worry about getting it. These were the days before mental illness happened.

There's undoubtedly nothing breathtaking about the following memory, but it remains one of the few I can cling to from a time when things were simple, and life made sense. I stand, not quite five years old, on the front porch of our house. It is the first day of kindergarten. I show my uncontainable excitement by simultaneously clapping, jumping, and chattering nonstop about everything coming to mind as I wait for the school bus.

Mom is taking numerous pictures while Andrew stands nearby. Dad has already left for work, but he will undoubtedly ask about my day when we gather at dinner that evening.

Despite a few innocent enough sibling rivalries, home life is carefree. My sensitivities are coddled in the bubble of our home. I manage to keep those around me pleased. Therefore, I feel a lot of the good emotion we all want to feel, the emotion we are supposed to feel - happiness.

I remember my first day of kindergarten vividly. The initial moments of it were filled with joyful anticipation. I looked forward to making new friends, learning to read, having lunch in the cafeteria, and of course, recess. Recess was incredibly awesome because we had an antique fire truck permanently parked on the playground. We jumped on the hood and played tag on the back (something a liability attorney would never allow now). It was incredibly fun - an absolute thrill for all of us.

After a few praises from teachers at school, something clicked. I quickly felt the expectations of the labeled "good girl" come to light - the girl who makes excellent grades and never gets in trouble. At first, it wasn't too difficult to maintain "pretty perfect," as my kindergarten teacher said of me.

Maybe it's the innocent brown eyes or the charming smile, but it's not the outward show that's so difficult to maintain. It will be the inner battles that flare in such a way that I cannot contain them.

Backyard Memories
April 1993

It is fair to say that we have the best backyard in the neighborhood. Dad builds us fun things, including a treehouse in the back of our one-acre lot. It stands twenty-five feet tall, wedged in the split of the branches of a stately tree. Well, maybe it is only twelve feet off the ground. Everything feels bigger as a child. Either way, it's incredible. We tie an ice cream bucket on one side. Mom slips "mail" and snacks in the bucket, and we hoist it up.

There are no rails on the treehouse; it's just understood not to be an idiot and fall off. My Brother is not an idiot, but somehow, he does manage to fall. His climbing skills take him past the treehouse until He reaches a branch that can't support him. He falls from the height of the treehouse plus a good ten feet. Seeing him unconscious and with the wind knocked out of him will remain a vivid memory. I run to get Mom. She holds him for a bit and says, "He will be just fine. The doctor wouldn't do anything. I'll just keep an eye on him."

That same treehouse has a zipline jutting out across the backyard, down a hill, and into another tree. Into another tree means, you will collide if you don't let go. It was also understood, don't be a moron and hit the tree. Society was a little different then, not so litigious. It was just kind of assumed that the neighbors wouldn't sue if their kid went smack dab into the tree trunk, which happened.

Despite a couple of mishaps, there are so many fond memories from that backyard. We rode that zipline more than we played with Christmas and birthday presents combined. Eventually, we would ride it so much that we would erode the entire pulley down to the center, finally rendering the zipline useless.

My brother, Andrew, and I play outside almost constantly. Physical pain is inevitable. Crashing my bike and landing on my face. Scraped knees. Falling off of monkey bars. Overall, these things are relatively minor and temporary. My experiences of pain are direct consequences of my carelessness, clumsiness, and occasionally an unforeseen accident. Physical pain makes sense to me; however, life would not always make sense. The emotional pain yet to come will rarely make sense at all.

Attempting to Out-Mow Mediocracy
August 1995

I am nine years old and broke, except for a few dollars tucked away in a piggy bank. I think most nine-year-olds are broke. But I take after my Dad. I want to work. I want to earn. I want to move up in this world.

It was never verbalized, but I learned my work ethic by watching my Dad work his tail off in the corporate world to get where he wanted to be. He travels often and works long hours. Even now in his sixties as a gray-haired grandpa, he can be found patching holes on the roof, insulating the basement, shoveling in the backyard to fix drainage pipes, and managing a full-time business.

Even when Dad is already as proud as he can be, I work extra hard to make him <u>more</u> proud. I pick up on the unspoken message that we can outrun our issues with enough effort. When life falls apart, work harder. And boom, problem solved.

I think this is one of the reasons mental illness will hit me so hard. There is no option to work one's way out of this. Maybe to a slight extent, but overall, nope.

Longing for cash and parental approval, I beg my parents for ways to make money. Dad makes a list (an Excel spreadsheet or as we call it, "Dad's love language") of the chores that can be done to earn money. These are in addition to the standard Saturday chores that are not for pay such as sweeping the kitchen, cleaning the bathrooms, washing the van, sweeping the garage steps, and filling the birdbath - tasks expected just for being part of the family.

The chores that are for pay include window washing. Theoretically, this one pays all right, but the problem lies with the time-consuming, endless critiquing by Dad and Mom. It is incredible how many streaks can be found when one looks from every possible angle. Because I am paid for task completion, the hourly pay is drastically decreased by their need to eradicate every streak.

I move on to another paying chore. I want to mow the lawn. My vision scans the spreadsheet to see that it will pay five dollars. This works out pretty well with a riding mower on an acre lot.

To put it kindly, Dad is very thorough. He pulls out the owner's manual for the lawnmower. He has made an examination to go along with it. Of course, he has. Before earning a penny, I must read every word in the stupid manual and pass the test. I jump through Dad's hoops and am finally ready to mow. Or so I think.

There are a couple of logistical issues to address. Problem number one: I am not tall enough to reach the pedal. Dad tapes a piece of sawed-off 2x4 to the pedal. This wood bridges the gap between my foot and the pedal.

I am finally off and mowing when I discover a second problem. The mower has a built-in safety mechanism. I'm sure it is to avoid mowing over people who have been ejected. The mower shuts off when there is no longer weight on the seat. Great design, but I don't weigh enough to stay on the seat when I hit a bump. I bounce with each rut or molehill, and the mower shuts off. I am constantly restarting it.

None of this stops me as I am hyper-focused on earning money and making progress. I am confident that I will be able to solve my problems in the world with hard work, dedication, and intelligence.

If only I knew that none of these remarkable qualities would ever be enough to protect me from the journey that lies ahead.

5th Grade Hall Patrol
October 1995

In addition to a good work ethic, I've always been sensitive, a peacekeeper, and the responsible one. This looked like being given tasks that other students were not given in school.

Only the finest students of the elementary school are given the responsibility of Hall Patrol. The job entails wearing an orange reflective vest and carrying a stack of tickets just waiting to be disbursed to the other students.

The Hall Patrol stands in designated areas at dismissal periods when children are generally happy to leave, thus running. In the case of any "speeders," tickets are to be written.

Innocent kindergarteners tremble at the thought of an offense. Hardened fifth-graders chuckle and make a game of escaping faster than a ticket can be produced.

Regardless, I am one of the few, the proud, the hall patrol.

Teachers have recommended me as a star pupil and worthy of the responsibility.

I coolly control the hallways while internally beginning to spiral out of control.

{growing up fast}

Eat Less to Control More
November 1995

At nine years old, I "should" be doing all the things I love, like painting my nails, reading Teen magazine, having sleepovers, and going to the movies. Instead, I get a glimpse of what living with (and hiding) a deep, mental pain feels like. It is about all that I can bear. I'm so glad that I am not aware this is just the tip of the iceberg. If I knew what was indeed coming, it would have been too much. One thing at a time. One day at a time.

The claws of mental illness begin to dig in at a young age.

I feel self-conscious and increasingly loathe some of my body. I begin anxiously weighing myself numerous times per day - terrified of gaining weight after every bite of food and swallow of liquid.

Any uncomfortable emotion is exchanged like currency, traded for fuel to achieve perfection.

I go about the school day spending the majority of the time comparing myself to the girls around me. My focus drifts away from classroom lessons onto the size of other girls' arms, legs, and stomachs. I find the skinniest girl in the class (the one who takes hours of ballet each day) and resolve to be like her, only thinner.

It doesn't take long to develop a foolproof plan - the only option for this desperate situation – a detrimentally strict diet. Vowing never to go over 900 calories per day, I read labels like a scrupulous detective, mentally calculating every tiny amount of caloric intake. I lie more and more, saying I've eaten already when I haven't and sneaking my food to the dog. My bedroom door

17

conceals hours of exercise. Others inspire me with their anorexia, proof that perfection can be achieved. It is my way of coping with the prickles and loneliness of the world.

Anorexia is my dreadful security blanket in a world that already seems too chaotic and frightening in fifth grade.

> Journal: "When I got home, Mom asked if I had eaten. I lied and said yes. I hated it, but I can't eat. I have lost a little weight and am now at 101! I want to be 95. I can do it. I promised myself I will not eat for 24 hours. I can only have diet drinks. I have done five hours. Oh wow! I have skipped ⅓ of the meals. I won't eat!"

Full-blown Anorexia in the Pilot's Seat
March 1998

My entire world revolves around food: wanting it so badly yet frantically trying to avoid it.

Anorexia has also struck two of my best friends, sucking the life out of what ought to have been our carefree childhoods. As I look at their sunken faces and emaciated arms, I see beauty. We participate in warped support, encouraging one another to refrain from the worst thing in the world – calories. I feel envious of their accomplishments. They frequently pass out, a side effect that positively reinforces well-done dieting. Their clothes drape off of their skeletal figures. One of them has been hospitalized. *I wish I had her motivation*. I've lost quite a few pounds as well, but I am still jealous of their more drastic achievements.

Conversely, I long for the mental peace I had before this phobia crept in. I need my mind to be quiet instead of constantly screaming, in fear, about gaining weight. It has gotten to the point where I can't retain my sanity and bear this burden alone. Anorexia is bigger than a kid-sized problem.

It's time to ask for help. Nicole, a friend from school, agrees to help me break the news to Mom. This is the biggest thing I have EVER had to tell anyone. It's terrifying, and I certainly don't dare to do it alone.

Nicole and I walk through the backyard with Mom. Nicole starts the conversation by cutting directly to the chase, "I think Leah is anorexic."

Mom listens calmly and attentively. In the most consoling voice, Mom says, "I could understand how this could happen. There is so much pressure about how we look."

I wish I could say that this would be the only time I'd need my parents to support me during distress. One can dream!

You Can't Choose Your Family
June 1997

Relatives come to visit every once in a blue moon. The closest family members are three states away. Others are continents away.

This family reunion is the first (and will turn out to be the last) for my Dad's side. We're all meeting in the middle – at

Grandma's and her new husband's place in Texas. We pile into the minivan and drive for fourteen hours.

Dad and Mom have told us for years that Uncle Greg had an accident. As we drive, they remind us of this and that his face looks different. It's a well-practiced plan. Prep the kids so they don't accidentally say anything rude or embarrassing. I am ten, old enough to know not to mention anything about Uncle Greg's face when I meet him.

Grateful to have finally arrived, we stretch our legs and take a good look around. It is a somewhat secluded lot with a nice-sized lake house. It is a short, beautiful stroll down to the water. At first glance, the most exciting things about the property seem to be the Texas-sized fire ant hills and an old fishing boat.

We start unpacking the van, grabbing suitcases, and heading for the house. Walking through the door, I gaze upon a room packed with people, all of whom I assume must be relatives. I feel sensory overload walking into this crowd of strangers. I mentally rehearse; which uncle goes with which aunt again? Which cousins are siblings?

Most of these are new faces, and it's always a little strange to meet relatives for the first time. With so little interaction, I struggle to keep everyone straight. It doesn't help that my grandparents thought it would be cute to choose names that all begin with G. There is Gary, Garth, Gil, Greg, and Gabrielle, to give you an idea.

My nervousness manifests as shyness.

I meet my cousin, Brandon. He is about seven years older than me. You can instantly tell he is one of the popular kids, from the way he carries himself to his stylish clothes and the windblown

20

hair of a movie star. My friends would be head-over-heels for him if they were along.

Next, I meet my little cousin Eric. He is four years old, and everyone comments on how adorable he is. It's true.

The meet and greet process continues as I gradually become more comfortable with these strangers to whom I happen to be related.

As a child, you don't understand the science of genetics. If I did, I would have looked around my family reunion and said, "Oh s*#%!" There is a great reason to be terrified. But I don't see it. Everybody else seems "normal." Laughing, storytelling, and a great time conceal their mental illness.

Then, I hear a loud voice, which long precedes the uncle it goes with. As he finally enters the room, I feel a punch-to-the-gut sense of shock. His face. Here is Uncle Greg. He is the one I was warned about. My attempt to be polite gives way to studying his face. It is unlike anything I've ever seen. He almost looks like Frankenstein. An extensive, jagged scar spans his forehead, with other more minor scars branching out. His nose looks like a tiny piece of putty that was haphazardly pushed on. One eye droops and continually drips tears. I now understand why Dad and Mom warned us.

Uncle Greg quickly transitions from introductions to divulging that he got in trouble on the bus ride here. My Brother, Andrew, and I wonder why but remain silent.

"I got in trouble for scaring a little kid on the Greyhound bus." Without any prompting, Uncle Greg takes it upon himself to demonstrate precisely why. He swiftly pops out an eyeball and then reaches for a cigarette lighter in his pocket. I'm still trying to process the initial shock that the eyeball is fake when he hits me with a double whammy; it can just pop out. I hear clink-clink-clink as Uncle Greg proceeds to tap the glass eyeball with the lighter in some bizarre attempt to impress us all.

Oh, my gracious. Who is this person? Yes, I am slightly traumatized, but even he does not raise any red flags about what could happen to ME. In my mind, he is an isolated incident. "

His dramatic acts continue. I overhear the adults saying he's making Elvis impressions again, but most of the humor is lost on me. I can't say I'm Elvis's number one fan or that I even know anything about him except that he died on a toilet. I force a smile while attempting to take it all in.

Uncle Greg's aberrant yet playful demeanor confuses me. His intense passion is unnerving. The frightening appearance of his face is hard to overlook.

I teeter between trying to like this sarcastic, outgoing uncle and attempting to deal with my uneasy gut feelings. I don't know what to make of Uncle Greg. I decide to observe a while longer.

It's day two of the family reunion. I am walking down the hallway past Uncle Greg. Without warning, he scoops me up in his arms, flips me upside down, and carries me by my ankles. I am far too big for this horseplay, but he takes me down the hallway to a bedroom anyway. The ceiling fan is circling above us. As my head is dangling near the floor, Uncle Greg tells me he is going to put my feet in the fan.

Terrified, I scream.

He laughs as he hoists me higher and higher until my toes are centimeters from the fan blades.

Just as suddenly as it started, he flips me upright, and it's over. Uncle Greg continues to laugh, seemingly unaware. Meanwhile, I'm in tears and don't find anything funny about this.

I tell my parents about the incident. They validate how frightening that must have been and attempt to comfort me. And they reveal Uncle Greg doesn't always make the best choices because of his brain.

I wonder what type of "accident" caused all of this. Through a process of internal dialogue, I answer my own question. It must have been a car accident, the only type of accident I can think of.

It is in the Semantics – "Accident"
July 1997

Time has passed since the family reunion, and specific incidents with Uncle Greg replay in my mind. The glass eye incident. Almost chopping my toes off in the fan. I just can't seem to make sense of him. Part of me feels intimidated and uncertain, which makes me thankful we live so far apart.

There's another part that couldn't be overlooked - how lighthearted he is, passing the time telling jokes and perfecting impersonations. It's undeniable he does love his family, openly hugging relatives and reiterating how thankful he was to have everyone together.

I've analyzed the family reunion over and over in my mind and obsessively dissected my interactions with Uncle Greg, but I can't figure him out.

In an attempt to clarify, I casually ask my parents a question I'm confident I know the answer to. "Uncle Greg had a car accident, right?" As soon as the words leave my mouth, Dad and Mom freeze. Their postures change as they scoot in close. *What is happening?*

My Dad is suddenly serious. In a somber tone, he explains, "Uncle Greg tried to kill himself with a gun. The bullet came out the front of his head, damaging his face and the front part of his brain. He has had a lot of surgeries on his face, and part of his brain is missing."

This revelation is my abrupt introduction to mental illness within our family.

Instantly, feelings of anger and betrayal well up inside of me. As tragic and shocking as this information is, all I can think is they have been lying to me for years. Uncle Greg did not have an accident. He tried to kill himself on purpose. I remain shocked and silent.

———————

Looking back, I see that being vague with the word "accident" was to avoid causing me distress. Now a parent myself, I know what it is like to want to protect my children from the tribulations of life. There is a difference between coddling and just wanting to avoid heartbreak.

Before speaking devastating news to my kids, I wonder, How can I spin this to make it less hurtful? What details can be left out to shield these innocent hearts? These are hard questions asked amid challenging situations. Often, the answer isn't clear. And no matter how much I try, heartache always manages to seep in.

That was all that my parents were trying to do. Protect my heart.

If One is Good, Three is Better.
The Motto of a Truly Stubborn, Sneaky, Go-getter.
March 1999

Eradicating anorexia is ridiculously difficult. Wanting treatment is synonymous with "getting fat" and much more complex than expected. Every meal brings up uneasy feelings. Wanting treatment sounds good until all of the control is gone, the emotions flood in, and a mirror reveals changes for the worse. It's not a linear course of treatment; it's riddled with many setbacks and more than a few fabrications.

Treatment now includes weekly visits with Dr. Perez (one of the top specialists in the area), counseling sessions, a consultation with a nutritionist, and an antidepressant. I guess it helps some. And when it doesn't, I lie and say it does.

Not to boast, but I think Dr. Perez likes me, professionally. I challenge him and keep him on his toes. He and his office staff have caught on to most of my tricks. They specialize in this kind of thing.

The nurse weighs me with my back to the scale, and no matter how much I beg and plead, she refuses to tell me the number. They know how much distress a change in body weight can cause. The nurse takes my vitals and leads me back to an exam room. This routine has become increasingly familiar.

I wait patiently, quietly listening to the white paper crunching beneath me on the exam table. A few minutes pass before Dr. Perez finally walks in the door with a stern look on his face.

He scolds, "Your resting heart rate is 181. What have you been taking?"

Oh, here we go. I guess Dr. Perez has figured out at least some of my latest schemes, a wonderful concoction of laxatives and diet pills. You have to be eighteen to purchase the good diet pills – the ones laced with Ephedra – but where there's a will, there's a way and no shortage of older guys walking through the mall to buy them for me at a nutrition store.

I've made a rookie mistake. Who would have thought diet pills could increase your heart rate that much?

I will only admit to one thing. It doesn't sound as bad in comparison to the whole truth, which actually includes an enormous amount of laxatives. "I've been taking diet pills."

He questions, "How many?"

I contemplate if I should answer this truthfully. I do. "The bottle said to take one three times a day, so I figured three pills three times a day would be better."

He rolls his eyes and makes a face. I can't tell if he's laughing or frustrated, or both.

He scolds, "You could have a heart attack."

At thirteen years old, I am not afraid of my heart quitting. I am afraid of being fat. I confidently reply, "We all have to die sometime."

Sometimes, dying sounds less frightening than living in fear and with pain.

The Introduction to Trauma and Beginning of Masking of Emotions
March 2000

Dawn is my best friend; We do everything together. Most of the time, that's a good thing, but occasionally, it is not. Today, we have agreed to meet up with some friends of a friend to buy some cocaine. I don't know why, but it sounds like a fun plan at the moment. Neither of us has tried it, and we are curious. I think it is fair to say that we both considered that we might break a couple of rules, but neither of us could have fathomed how traumatic the day would become.

Dawn parks the car at the nearest side street, adjacent to the scheduled location. As we get out of the car, two guys approach us. We quickly realize that we have been set up.

One of the guys points at me.

"I have a gun. If you want to live, you'll do exactly what I tell you to do. And if you tell anyone, I'll kill your family."

My body trembles. I beg for him to stop, but it is to no avail. I offer all of the cash in my wallet.

He refuses it. "I don't want the money. I want you. You are the prettier of the two."

I do what he says, whatever it takes to remain alive. I hope that cooperating will save Dawn from whatever is about to occur to me.

It works. Dawn remains safe with the other guy. On the other hand, I am led to a gravel section of a cemetery where I endure a violent sexual assault.

The events of that day would replay over and over for years to come. If only... I should have... Get over it. The world's evil expressed through that degree of trauma would remain bottled up, corroding my fourteen-year-old soul. This day would mark the pendulum shift, when the world would no longer be primarily good but instead mainly evil.

I wish I could tell someone else about the events of this life-altering day, someone who could help. But what choice do I have?

My Mom does notice later that day. "Why are your knees bleeding?"

His voice replays in my head, "If you tell anyone. I'll kill your family."

I lie to Mom. "I tripped." My chance for help is gone. I bottle up the pain in an attempt to save the ones I love.

———————

I've heard of the assignment to write a letter to your younger self. If you could tell that child a few things, what would they be? I would write my letter to myself as I lay my head on my pillow at the end of this horrific day.

Leah, as grown as you think you are, this is not a child-sized problem. Please, reach out for adult help. You will be believed. You will not be blamed. You did nothing to deserve this. Even if you were up to mischief, this is not your fault. You do not need to carry this burden alone. You are loved and just as treasured as always.

My world is forever altered. I struggle to keep up the facade that I am fine and dandy.

The (Delicate) Art of Getting One's Act Together
February 2002

Concerning the eating disorder, Dr. Perez is happy with my progress. The anorexia symptoms are nearly gone, and I've been discharged from his care. However, there's also quite a bit Dr. Perez doesn't know (that no adults know). What I've really learned, and what truly helped the eating disorder, is that guys like curves more than skin and bones. So, there is the boyfriend and the pills. The smoking. The drinking.

From the outside, I am beginning to look very much like a "troubled teen" or a "rebellious, spoiled brat." The truth is that the extreme hurt I am constantly feeling makes every moment of the day seem unbearable. My search for inner peace looks a lot like self-medicating and poor decision-making.

I've used my shape and sex appeal to lure in one of the most popular upper-classmen I never dreamed I could get. We have been together for a high school eternity: three months.

Prescription pain medications numb all types of pain; I'm looking mainly for relief from emotional pain. I don't want to remember the rape from two years ago. But it's more than that. I've never been good at dealing with any emotions. For almost as long as I can remember, life has been prickly and painful. Now, the pain of life is too intense to handle alone, without the comfort of substances. Self-medicating takes me from a sensitive perfectionist

29

to a badass, capable of handling anything. (Anything except withdrawal, of course.)

I walk down the hallways of the school smiling and maintaining straight A's, keeping the secret of what it takes for me to function. I have my regiment: diet pills in huge quantities, Lortabs, Vicodins, and Xanax when my mind won't stop. Alcohol when I need an escape, or a disguise of happiness. Vodka in a water bottle makes school more tolerable. And anything extra to pop or drink is greatly appreciated. I don't want to be high, but I just can't handle the discomforts of life.

There is one thing I seem to be managing well - my romantic relationship. It's an easy formula: sex and more sex. However, something is missing from the formula that neither the boyfriend nor I considered in the heat of the moment – protection.

Now, I'm stuck, waiting for a period that doesn't appear to be coming.

I make it to the drug store to steal the pregnancy test. It is $8, which is $8 more than I have to my name. I have spent most of my money on clothes to be popular and pills to function.

Oh my God. Two lines. Pregnant.

Terrified of my uber-religious parents, I come up with the best plan my fifteen-year-old brain can conceive. I will kill myself in the bathtub by overdosing on a few Tylenol. I will go unconscious and drown so my parents will never find out.

I take the pills, get in the tub, and slam my head as hard as possible into the back of the tub, hoping to blackout.

After a massive, self-inflicted blow to the head, I do blackout, but only for a millisecond. When I open my eyes, I find I am still very much alive, just with a throbbing headache.

I plan for days, trying to conjure up anything else to avoid my parents finding out. Ah-ha, I will do what all the other pregnant, snooty girls at school do - get an abortion. Too young to go on my own, another classmate's mother agrees to take me to the clinic. She is known for not caring – frequently buying alcohol for children (Well, until she would eventually lose custody of them). We figured she'd be down for this too, and she is. The appointment is scheduled for that Friday.

It is Tuesday, and I need $500 fast. I have watched my mother enter the pin on her debit card at the grocery store for years. I need access to the card. I sneak in her purse and pluck the card out. From there, I make it to the bank, get the money, and head home to replace the card and act like everything is fine.

Inside I am terrified. Terrified of my parents. Afraid of getting an abortion. Scared of not getting an abortion. Terrified in every conceivable way.

Wednesday comes. My parents casually mention in a creepily calm voice that they have been the victims of identity theft. In my best-collected, yet internally petrified voice, I offer condolences and go on about my business. How much do they know?

Later in the day, Dad and Mom sit me down and explain matter-of-factly that the bank ensures the card. The bank will watch the video footage and plan to press felony charges, including bank robbery and identity theft, against the perpetrator.

31

I burst into tears. Backed into a corner, I explain I am pregnant, and my abortion is in two days. I needed money for it.

My parents hug me. I still don't know how, but they don't freak out. Once again, they are weird and handle big stuff better than the small daily things. They convey that they won't allow me to get an abortion because of their beliefs, but they will support me as we explore other options.

The Start of Maternal Instincts I Never Knew I Had
March 2002

The next few weeks are horrific. I quit my entire pain-numbing and self-directed mood-stabilizing techniques at once. The vodka and the pills, and even the cigarettes are gone. I shake, rock, hurt, and throw up. I know this baby can't handle the substances. This is cold-turkey dealing with life, and it sucks.

As the magnitude of the pregnancy sinks in, my high school sweetheart is already fading out of the picture. I feel the pressure of this weighty decision resting solely upon my shoulders. Am I capable of raising a tiny human when I'm failing at just being a teenager? Highly doubtful.

Dad and Mom take me to an appointment with an adoption agency. It sounds like the best plan yet. As I fill out numerous pages of paperwork, I barely notice the question related to race - one of many questions. I answer truthfully, checking two boxes: Caucasian and African American.

I finish filling out the paperwork as a caseworker enters the room. We chat for a while. Honestly, I don't remember anything we talk about except for the end, the part when she tells me she cannot guarantee placement because Caucasian babies are the most sought after.

Suddenly, a maternal instinct I never knew I had rages. Who wouldn't want a precious baby because he is biracial? That is the stupidest reason I've ever heard. I wouldn't trust such people with my baby anyway. There is no reason I can't get myself together and raise this baby, even if I have to do it alone!

That's all it took, the threat of not being able to find placement for my baby. From that point on, I was determined to make it work on my own.

> Journal: "My boyfriend is thinking that when I tell him I am keeping the child, if that's what I decide, then he is leaving. He said we could not be together because I would not be thinking of our relationship. And in that case, why should he? He says he has a life to live, no financial support, and isn't ready to emotionally support a child. I agree with that, and I realize I'm not ready for this either. I think where we disagree is when it comes to if we could or would grow up quickly because we need to. He wants to be a kid - play soccer, mess up in school, and chill with his friends. I am willing to grow up quickly to accept responsibility. He wants to have as little responsibility as possible."

An Indisputable Belly
August 2002

It's nearly impossible to remain the token "good girl" as my abdomen is now undeniably protruding from my small teenage frame.

Before, it was relatively easy to portray different facets of me, a straight-A, responsible young lady to parents and teachers; another who could always give the correct answer at church; and yet another rebellious personality with friends. The pregnancy experience is the first time these various and incongruent traits have converged into one struggling, confused, and petrified girl.

The most logical next step in this fiasco seems to be looking for a job, although at fifteen and pregnant, I'm not the ideal candidate.

Shockingly, the last person I would have expected, the women's director at a church, Victoria, offers me a little work. I'll be starting with a once-a-week childcare job. I'm skeptical of how religious fanatics will receive me, but the need for money overpowers my fear of rejection, so I take the job.

Along with a few other girls, I help with kids while their parents are in Wednesday night bible studies. A few weeks go by, and it's not too bad; I actually enjoy it.

This evening, just as every other night I've worked, I walk down the hallway into my assigned room. Fully expecting children, I am stunned as a room full of women jump out screaming, "Surprise! Happy Birthday!" Totally caught off guard, I scan the room noticing a few familiar and even more new faces.

Is this for my birthday? It is my 16th birthday, but what in the world is going on?

I notice a giant, tall-as-me pyramid. A pyramid made of boxes of diapers and wipes. It is as if someone transported pallets of baby products from Costco. Sensing my confusion, Victoria explains that women in the church have all chipped in to get me a year's supply of diapers and wipes. To celebrate my birthday, they've all conspired to throw me this surprise party.

I expected judgment from this religious community that I hardly knew. Instead, I was welcomed beyond my wildest imagination and shocked beyond belief. I feared my prayers for provision for my baby had gone unheard, but I couldn't deny the blessing I barely had room enough to receive.

_____

The diapers would last a year, and the last package of wipes would run out the week this little one would become potty trained.

Two in the Driver's Seat
September 2002

Finally eligible for a driver's license, I waddle, 33 weeks pregnant, into the DMV to take the driver's test. After filling out the necessary paperwork, an employee accompanies me to the car. The seatbelt is extra tight around my expansive waistline. I try to ignore the reality of how short my arms feel and how large my stomach truly is, even making it difficult to reach the steering wheel.

I wonder what the lady administering the test is thinking about me. She keeps it professional as she focuses on her clipboard, checking boxes and jotting down notes. She doesn't have to say anything. It is humiliating, but I remind myself that this, too, is a necessary step toward providing for this baby.

I use turn signals, come to complete stops, and follow every speed limit. I am granted a driver's license a couple of days after my sixteenth birthday, just weeks before I'll become a mother.

The Day That Makes Me a Mama
October 2002

At 39 weeks, I go into labor. All goes smoothly with the delivery - epidural, pushing, and boom - a 9 lb 12 oz baby boy, Jordan. I wake up as a teenager and go to bed as a mother. It is a lot to take in. I hold him tight, studying his precious fingers and toes, caressing his curly hair, and reiterating how tiny he is. The nurses disagree with the "tiny" part and jokingly call him "Pork Chop."

Jordan is precious and truly helpless. Feelings of needing to become stable as quickly as possible consume me. He deserves the best. The only way to give him the best is to go faster and harder. I don't have any time to waste.

I value education as the ticket to a better life. Jordan is born on a Wednesday, and by the following Monday, I am back in class.

Journal: "I am sitting in the baby's room breastfeeding the most beautiful baby in the world. His name is Jordan. A week ago, I went to the doctor for a

36

checkup. He stripped my membranes, which is supposed to help you go into labor. He had done it the week before, and it didn't do anything so, I wasn't expecting too much. I started getting cramps and stuff but didn't worry about it. I went to school in the morning. I asked my principal at lunch if I could go home because my tummy was hurting. Dad came and got me. We went for a walk because I couldn't get comfortable. We started timing the contractions - seven minutes apart. Mom came home from bible study, and we got ready to go. I took a shower and packed the rest of my bag. I checked into the hospital at four o'clock. I was 6 centimeters so I got an epidural right away. I was seven centimeters at eight o'clock, and the doctor broke my water. A bunch of people showed up in my room. We had a little party until eleven when it was time to push. Even with the epidural, I could move my legs and feel the urge to push. At 11:52 p.m., he was born. He has a nice head full of hair. I love him to death! I just look at him for as long as I can! He has got to be the sweetest baby in the whole world. Well, I gotta go to sleep because I have to go to school for a few hours in the morning. It will come early, especially with him waking up during the night."

Busy Is An Understatement
January 2003

The role of mother comes quite naturally, but it's certainly not the only hat I have to wear. I make every minute count - juggling school, studying, and more babysitting gigs. I'm blessed that my Mom has agreed to watch Jordan while I am at school. Other than that, Jordan is along for everything, including evening babysitting.

Jordan provides what was missing, a reason to get emotionally healthier. He gives a purpose for this season of striving. Jordan is my "Why?" and motivates me to clean up my act.

Get In and Get Out
May 2003

I've done some finagling. The school district has given me the approval to do my junior and senior high school years together while simultaneously taking some college courses. The concern for the future allows nothing less than operating at warp speed.

As high school graduation approaches, I don't rank in my class because I am not technically supposed to graduate for another year. The principal nudges my arm, "You sure you don't want to stay? You have the highest GPA in your class and will be valedictorian if you wait around."

I chuckle. "I don't need to be valedictorian."

I am worried about getting off to college to find a job to take care of this little guy. My motherly instincts are in full effect; I've made my mind up, and there's no convincing me otherwise.

It also doesn't help that I suffered a striving perfectionist's worst nightmare - the public humiliation of teen pregnancy. I'm off to repair the image and regain admiration as well.

Home is Where Love Resides
August 2004

I've saved enough money from babysitting and am legally old enough to move out. I've been looking forward to this day for quite some time. There are too many weird dynamics accompanying being parented in your family home while trying to parent your own little one. Ugh! My independent spirit has been stifled, and it's time for a new chapter.

The new spot isn't fancy, but it is perfect for Jordan and me. An old, historic house has been divided into a triplex, each section of the rental with totally separate living spaces and entrances. We occupy the far left strip with a living room, kitchen, bedroom, bathroom, and laundry room. It couldn't be more than 500 square feet, but I am ecstatic!

I rapidly accumulate furniture from garage sales and thrift stores. A second-hand sofa is refreshed with a red, faux suede slipcover. With a fresh coat of white paint, a dingy kitchen table looks clean and crisp. The laundry room is barely big enough to squeeze in Jordan's car-shaped toddler bed. I spend countless hours proudly organizing and decorating, making this little spot our own. It is perfect!

Adulting
October 2004

I've heard rumors about how difficult it is to be a grownup. That's just not my experience. Adulting comes easier than I expected. It doesn't take long to learn how to budget, pay bills on time, keep a clean house, and cook healthy dinners. I learn to hang curtains and snake drains. I even send grinning Christmas photos to everyone we know – if that doesn't prove how well we are doing, nothing can.

This is the epitome of being a productive member of society and a positive parent. This is what it's like to have your act together.

I may have started rocky and a little young, but no one would question how well Jordan and I are doing now.

The stability is welcomed. I imagine life will always be this calm.

Career Choices
August 2005

I genuinely enjoy the kids I babysit; however, I'd like something steadier. I've finished all the general courses I can take at the community college. I can waiver no longer; I must decide on the next course of action.

The medical field fascinates me, and I've always loved the idea of helping people. Sciences are my strengths. I am naturally curious about the human body, always wondering, What causes this? How does that work? What do you do in a medical emergency?

Initially, I set out to be a doctor. It takes only one semester of pre-med to determine there is not enough time to go to medical school as a single parent. I must find something to start earning money sooner, and it must pay enough for us to live independently. I finally decided an associate's degree in nursing could work.

I hear people talk about a nursing shortage. There is a high demand for nurses, but the schools have limited spots. I take my chances at one of the best schools around, a private Catholic nursing school.

I assemble the application packet and write out a check for the small application fee. I drop it off with one of the nuns working in the administration building.

Weeks go by before I finally find out I've been placed on the extensive waiting list. My heart sinks. The waiting list is better than a "No," but it doesn't help me get out into the workforce any sooner.

I've come to accept, for whatever reason, the timing must not be right. I've even forgotten that today is the day before classes start.

Oddly enough, I get a phone call from the college. Someone has missed the deadline to pay for classes. Their spot has now become available. I feel terrible for the person who has been purged, but I am thrilled about getting into the program.

This door has opened, an opportunity I won't take for granted. I start the next day.

Private, Catholic nursing school as a single parent of a little one is a challenge, but even so, I manage to excel.

At graduation, I don my cap and gown. Then, someone hands me the weirdest thing. "Why are you giving me a rope?" I learn that this is called an "honor cord," and I've earned it for my good grades. I see nursing as my ticket out of struggling and a guarantee for a stable life.

Not Old Enough for a Glass of Wine But Giving IV Meds
June 2006

It is nearly three o'clock in the morning. I join the security guard, respiratory therapist, and clinical supervisor and step into the elevator. At nineteen years old, I feel the weight of my first nursing job as a cardiac care nurse. Tonight, I am training as part of the Code Team. The security guard turns the key in the elevator as he firmly presses the button for the hospital's roof. There is small talk amongst the staff as we rise.

The doors open, and we step out onto the dark roof. It is a fantastic view of the entire city from up here. We wait and absorb the eerie silence. After a few minutes, the sound of a helicopter pierces the quiet. Our life-flight patient is almost here.

Inwardly, I am nervous, but I know I was made to do this. I was one of the youngest, if not the youngest, to complete the school's nursing program. I remember the pages of the textbooks with an almost photographic memory. When a disease is mentioned, I mentally picture the paragraph and location on the page.

I take pride in working hard, even when it means skipping a meal or bathroom break. I notice the tiny changes in the patients'

42

conditions others might overlook. I even heard a doctor whisper to his patient, "You got Leah, the best nurse."

Per hospital policy, we wait for the chopper blades to stop. It isn't as glamorous as the movies portray, and it is undoubtedly more nerve-wracking. We run over, transferring the patient out of the helicopter. We continue attending to him as we hop on the elevator and rush down the hospital hallways to an open ICU bed.

I hurry back to the cardiac care unit, where my patients are waiting for me. The nurses are great about covering each other's patients during an emergency. I am so thankful for the camaraderie because the Code Team pager goes off three more times before the night is over.

By 7:15 a.m., I am exhausted. I have done chest compressions for longer than the average workout class. The high acuity, fast-paced, and sleep deprivation are draining, but this is my element. I drink a cup of coffee before starting my 45-minute commute home to Jordan. The events of the night replay in my mind as I go through the motions of my drive home.

As a nurse, I am confident in my critical care skills, but I had just about the most basic training in mental health. Our class spent a few weeks rounding in the state psychiatric hospital. I spent time sitting on the floor with an individual in a catatonic state. I had a fascinating conversation with another patient who informed me that he "was not from around here" and that it took him "a week on a starship to get here."

I got just enough hands-on hours paired with a semester in the classroom to get me what I would need to know how to pass the licensure exam. However, this training would not provide enough for what I would need for life.

A textbook can't fully explain the feeling of a debilitating panic attack. I had no idea how a manic episode would present itself. I could have never dreamed of the depths of depression. But I would learn.

{is this "normal?"}

Pressing Home Improvement
July 2007

At this point, I have a full-time job, a mortgage, and a three-year-old, and it comes pretty naturally for me to do what has to be done. Others seem a little surprised, like the guy who prepared the closing documents on the house. I guess it isn't typical to buy a home at nineteen, but I'm thankful life is coming together. I think I've finally found it – normal.

I am ecstatic to be in this new house. We have space and freedom, and it is lovely. It doesn't require much maintenance since it is only a year old. I plant a few shrubs and paint the living room walls. We slowly settle in, getting everything we need from the lawnmower to the bedroom set to artwork for the walls. I take my time, doing what I can with each paycheck. The home is really coming together.

Seemingly out of nowhere, I get the feeling we need tiles around the garden tub in the main bathroom. I hadn't thought of this until now, but I can't wait. This is CRITICAL! I must leave now, or Home Depot will close before I can get the supplies I need.

Thankfully, they are open until 10:00 p.m. I start picking out inexpensive materials that look like they will get the job done.

I've never worked with tile in my life, and this is in a time before YouTube tutorials, although I don't know that I could slow down long enough to watch one anyway. The cheapest tiles are white subway tiles. Perfect. This is such a great plan. I grab some mortar, white grout mix, a hand tile cutter, and a few tools. Even though none of this was in the budget, I justify the project by reminding myself how much money I am saving by doing it myself. It must be done, so this is the way to go.

Full of energy, I irreverently speed home. While most of the neighbors are turning out the lights for the night, I am just getting started. There is no time to waste by reading directions or worrying about technique. I cover the walls and, inadvertently myself, in all kinds of sticky and powdery substances. I eyeball the tile placement, never considering spacers. I cut the end and corner tiles by hand.

It is now mid-morning, and the project turned out surprisingly well. I have been up all night and would like to get some rest. My knees hurt from kneeling on the hard bathroom floor. My hands ache from the stupid, cheap tile cutter. My back is sore from bending over.

I am physically exhausted, but my mind is racing faster and faster.

I have an urgent realization that the kitchen needs a tile backsplash. I cannot rest at a time like this. Like a puppet controlled by frantic thoughts, complying with the demands of my first (unrecognized) manic episode, I head back to Home Depot for more supplies.

My Early Twenties, A Record Low
2008

I wish I could give an exact account of my life – precisely how things fell apart; However, this is where the holes in my memory become even more prominent. It was a little patchy before, but these gaps are undeniably vacant. It's not only that my memory is faulty – this is when the severe mental illness strikes with numerous hospitalizations and multiple suicide attempts leading to electroconvulsive therapy (ECT) treatments that will erase vast chunks of my memory.

This period includes jumping into a marriage (which will quickly become unhealthy). I don't remember any details about the extravagant wedding, Caribbean honeymoon, or even the pregnancy with a new baby, Micah. I vaguely remember filing for divorce.

I am missing major life events and memories of the day-in/day-out routines.

I've written what I know, but there are gaping holes spanning nearly a decade.

Eye Movement Desensitization and Reprocessing
August 2009

I sit in the waiting room of a non-profit counseling center with my head held low and my mind deep in thought. My fresh start is tainted with confusion and fear. Traumatic memories replay in my mind like a vivid movie on repeat.

I don't know what is real anymore. I don't trust anyone or anything, not even myself. How much of this despair is justified? How would the average person respond to finding out their marriage is not salvageable? How do people handle starting over as a broke, single parent?

My new diagnoses of postpartum depression and post-traumatic stress disorder coincide with the crumbling of my marriage. The fighter in me is going to need to work overtime. I am losing the ability to pull it all together or even fake that it is pulled together. My mind continues to think of everything I wish I had done differently. Every pivotal point that could have led to a better outcome won't escape my mind.

This mental rehashing is interrupted by the counselor's soft, compassionate voice - the kind that makes you wonder if she ever yells in traffic or screams at her kids. She asks, "Are you ready to go up?" I pick up my gray leather purse and follow her upstairs to her office. I sit down on the loveseat as she scoots her wingback chair a little closer to me.

Today, we are starting something new – eye movement desensitization therapy (EMDR). After chatting about the week, she opens a laptop showing me the screen, and giving instructions. I feel cautiously optimistic – hoping for relief, all the while questioning if my symptoms are beyond repair.

Romantic Bull's-Eye
October 2009

After multiple failed relationships with men, I seem to have subconsciously developed an unhealthy relationship with shopping. When I am down and lonely (which is happening more and more), Target picks me up. I finally get out of my pajamas and fix my hair. The allure of hope – the newness of life the store has to offer - greets me. The red and white bulls-eye serves as a beacon advertising peace. My worries melt away as I walk through the sliding doors to grab a shopping cart. Even the knowledge of my mounting credit card debt becomes a distant memory.

But it's not only when I'm down. The store is my knight in shining armor, solving practically everything. The store aisles are happy to support me during times of energy when my mind is racing with "urgent" things to acquire. The beautiful textures and patterns capture my complete attention. I take hours meticulously studying the shelves of each aisle, admiring and comparing. I lift the lids smelling each candle until I get a headache. My senses are consumed with the stimulation of the store, and for a moment, the deafening thoughts racing through my mind are muted.

Shopping has become my solution to almost every problem. Jordan jokes, "Target is your boyfriend because you love it so much." I am there hours a day, multiple times a week, spending hundreds of dollars a visit. I certainly can't afford one more thing, so I go shopping to numb the pain of not being able to afford one more thing. I attempt to hide new purchases and often lie about where I've been.

I can't make it through the pain of daily life without companionship, so I look to the one true love that remains. I buy things with the hope of finding the joy that I have yet to attain in any other way. My spending habits represent the lack of control that engulfs my life.

{all hell breaks loose}

Not Immune
November 2009

This is when it happens. Doing the adult thing well – it detonates. I can't fathom doing the things I used to do. Mustering the energy for house cleaning or lawn care is out of the question. I don't cook anymore. I hide, longing to go unnoticed, withdrawing from most around me and all forms of social media. I want to fall off the map to avoid others witnessing my demise.

It's bewildering how I manage to lose so much in such a short time. My job is infeasible as I'm too depressed to show up on time (or often at all). The divorce is pending. I'm not sure how much was my fault versus his fault; regardless, even the best counselors can't salvage the relationship. The illusion of a happy, healthy family is shattered. My house, the one I love and have worked for, is advertised in the local papers – foreclosure – for all to see that I'm also financially unstable.

My external life is crumbing, while I'm becoming increasingly unstable internally. I don't remember the day when my diagnosis changed, but the doctors swap it from "depression" or some sort of "postpartum funk" to "severely bipolar." I'm labeled Bipolar Not Otherwise Specified (NOS) Rapid Cycling with Psychotic Features.

This is where life and the mounting symptoms of sorrow and stress become too much. I increasingly listen to the negative emotions, following thoughts as imperative commands. I decide temporary measures are not numbing the pain. I will need a more permanent solution – suicide.

I've embarked on a treacherous journey with mental illness.

Storm Cloud's a Brewin'
January 2010

The commercials that depict depression as a small gray cloud following someone down a sidewalk make me want to vomit. If it were only that small and simple, maybe I could get over it by trying harder and flexing my mental muscles to overpower this little, gloomy fluff of cotton.

Severe depression is more like a black sky apocalypse. My mind says cancel everything. Hide. It is all too much. Sleep and conserve energy. Even the slightest task of showering is overwhelming and takes two days of mental cheerleading to make it happen. All of my plans for the future are likely to fail, and I am afraid of rejection. Even a smiling face is intimidating. It emphasizes what others have that I don't – joy. Sometimes depression creeps in slowly. Other times it bombards unannounced. However it arrives, despair replaces hope.

Thoughts repeat you will never get out of this state. Your life will forever be miserable if you choose to continue. Here is where enduring begins to lose its appeal. There are no words, and indeed, no commercials, that can portray the anguish of deep depression.

From Provider to Patient
February 2010

Without warning, gut-wrenching sobbing has started and continues without any end in sight. Day after day, the tears pour heavily from deep within. I struggle to manage the psychological pain. My depression has been bad in the past but never this bad. I am not okay. This warrants my first in-patient medication adjustment, my first trip to the mental hospital.

I don't know what to expect. I vacillate between wondering what the hospital's psychiatric wing will be like and being so caught up in my pain that I don't care. I can't imagine a more uncomfortable place than inside my mind.

After being checked in by the staff in the psychiatric unit, there is a period of vulnerability and uncertainty. I am the new admit with no knowledge of how this place works or who any of the other patients are. It's exponentially more frightening than the first day in a new school.

I don't want to be alive, and I certainly don't want to spend my forced life here.

Another part of my psyche counters, *I don't belong here. I have to get back to my children. I have to get back to nursing. I am supposed to be the provider, not the patient.*

I'm concerned others will find out about my hospitalization. I worry this admission will negatively affect the custody arrangement during the pending divorce hearings. I resolve to do what the hospital staff wishes and tell them what they want to hear to get out of this place.

As I timidly make my way to a chair in the day room, the other patients seem equally, if not more, curious about me than I am about them. Invasive questions are asked without any reservation, "Why are you here?" and "What is your diagnosis?" After a while, I become used to the questions and realize they demonstrate concern and establish confidants.

There isn't the same level of privacy here as there is in other hospital units - the units I am familiar with from working. Here, there are two patients in a room sleeping in adjacent twin beds. Vitals are taken publicly in the day room. Everyone waits in line for medications to be dispersed from a little wooden half-door at the nurses' station.

I begin to learn more about the other patients in the unit. Some individuals are so sedated they cannot function, drooling and falling asleep sitting up. Others are volatile, making scenes with short tempers and physical violence. One guy starts punching holes in the drywall next to the locked doors of the unit. After a failed attempt to verbally calm him down, the staff swoops in with a tranquilizing shot.

A few patients just seem to have hit a rough patch and obsess about getting back to their families and jobs. I meet another lady who is here for a suicide attempt following a diagnosis of Parkinson's disease. An occasional person is here faking symptoms for some sort of personal gain. For example, one lady who stays across the hall from me says she has eighteen personalities, but I hear the staff whispering that she is malingering. Some people have dual diagnoses. I watch one patient suffering from severe withdrawal symptoms snort the coffee grounds from the dayroom coffee pot in an attempt to find even the slightest alleviation of discomfort. Other patients are known as the frequent fliers, the people who can't make it outside of these walls for long.

I want to be the "rough patch" type of patient, believing this will resolve quickly, and I will be back to life, as I knew it. I fully understand my diagnosis while continuing to cling to my identity as a nurse. Now, I am on the other side. I continually rely on my past accomplishments in an attempt to prove I do not fit in here. Somehow, I hope a productive past will cushion my future.

Camp Kooky
February 2010

I've finally figured out what this place reminds me of. The mental hospital is like a summer camp, only with unstable campers. Although my roommate and I aren't on rustic, wooden bunk beds, we share a room with mattresses thin enough to feel the bedsprings. We wake to the sound of a counselor summoning us out of our rooms and rounding up our unit for breakfast. When we arrive in the cafeteria on schedule, we must sit with members of our floor, not any of the other units. Except for a few intermittent periods of free time, the remainder of the day is tightly structured.

Everyone takes turns using one phone on the wall, much like waiting in line to call home at the end of a long day in the summer heat. It never fails that someone feels the need to be a self-appointed secretary, fielding all incoming phone calls during the allotted phone times. The only difference is that this phone is unplugged at the jack and taken off the wall during group sessions.

As I watch the other patients, I notice that the formed relationships remind me of summer camp. There is a bond, which seems to build regardless of our differing mental states, much more quickly than it does in the outside world. We're all in this together. It is not uncommon to hear people sharing astonishingly personal, graphic stories you wouldn't feel comfortable sharing anywhere else. At discharge, people act as if they are leaving a new best friend, giving drawn-out parting speeches and (despite rules prohibiting it) phone numbers to keep in touch.

I keep to myself, hoping no one asks for my number. I enjoy the company while I am held here, but I don't feel the need to stay connected after this. I have to return to my real world and leave this strange psychiatric camp behind.

We wrap up the day with evening medications and mandatory lights-out time. The counselors and nurses stay in the hallways to ensure we remain in our rooms until the next morning's wake-up call.

The Golden Ticket Out of Here
February 2010

I quickly learn there is a simple formula for getting out of the psychiatric hospital. I fervently deny all suicidal ideations. I reiterate my plans for dealing with depression or crisis in the future, citing names of people I will call on for help, and I promise not to stockpile medications. I attend group meetings and insert at least one or two comments to display my active participation. I walk circles around the gym during the afternoon activity time.

It doesn't take long to get discharged with impeccable behavior and insurance regulations. I am sent home with little change in my internal thought process, a follow-up appointment, and a new concoction of medications.

Searching for an Escape
February 2010

The vow against stockpiling doesn't last long. Each pill collected represents a bit of hope eroded. It will be these actions and the loss of hope that result in multiple suicide attempts, including the one mentioned at the beginning of the book.

The same scenario plays out over and over. I lack coping skills and want to quit on life. Medical staff intervenes on my unconscious body. I spend time in critical care before being transferred to a psychiatric unit. Somehow, despite my deepest longings to end the pain, I pull through.

It would be damn near a decade before the deeply rooted beliefs fueling the suicide attempts would change.

A Glimpse of Perspective
March 2010

Somewhere amidst my own pain and suffering, I get news about Aunt Gabrielle. My Dad's only sister has taken her life. I am too emotionally drained to know how to handle this news. It is tragic. I can't even imagine what my cousin is going through losing his Mom. I picture Eric's cute little four-year-old face from the family reunion. Even now (not four but still so young), he is only in high school. No one should ever have to go through that.

Instantly, my mind comes to a screeching halt. You almost put your kids through that.

The mental debates continue. The pendulum swings from jealousy that Aunt Gabrielle's pain has ended while I'm left here to struggle to thinking that I am the lucky one. I'm able to get help and stick around long enough to get a glimpse of a brighter future.

It is nearly impossible to know how to process all of this from a profoundly depressed perspective. It is at this time that I begin to understand the genetic aspect of my illness. Out of self-preservation, I try to think about her death as little as possible, at least until I am healthier myself.

Frequent Flyer
April 2010

Hospitalizations are becoming increasingly frequent, an almost ordinary event occurring at least once a month. Multiple attempted overdoses continuously prove I've simply lost the ability to cope with the struggles of life.

It all feels like too much. Even the most straightforward task leads to a pervasive feeling of being overwhelmed. I have lost the ability to process emotions competently. They've been blocked and filtered for so long that I'm left with only two extreme options: happy or suicidal.

I start accumulating the "frequent flier" title I tried so desperately to avoid.

My Mother's Presence, Until We Are Separated
June 2010

Mom and I walk through the front doors of the psychiatric hospital. The staff greets us with questions.

"Can I help you? What seems to be going on?"

I reply, "I am feeling suicidal, and my doctor wants me here." My speech and movements are slow. I cry because I don't have the energy to put the pain into words. My chest physically hurts from days of sobbing.

My mother and I are escorted to a tiny room with a stretcher and a chair: no picture frames, no decorations, nothing that could be adapted into a harmful object.

Mom is a calming presence. She conceals her own emotions to be solid for me.

A security guard joins us. "Ma'am, I need to search your bags. Is there anything sharp that could poke me?" I shake my head no. I've learned better than to pack a razor. I brought flip-flops instead of shoes with laces. My hoodie is still missing the drawstring from the last admission. It is an uneventful search.

We continue to wait. The caseworker is making phone calls and arranging for my admission. I appreciate Mom's company, but we don't talk. There isn't much to say. We have been here many times before.

Hours have passed, and it is almost midnight. There is finally a bed available. I hug Mom before she heads for the front door. The employee leads me in the opposite direction to a locked unit.

The admission nurse methodically swipes her badge to open the double doors. As we walk onto and through the unit, I hear the sound of the metal doors firmly closing. They separate me from the general population. The doors demarcate the free and the mentally ill.

When I arrive, it is late, and the lights are low. The patients are all in their rooms. The psychiatric nurses are gathered behind desks and charting on computers. There is a quick exchange of words. "This is Leah, your new admit."

The nurses continue the admission process. After a long series of questions I could recite by heart, I am ushered to a room. I sneak into bed as quietly as possible so as to not wake my new roommate.

To Visit or Not to Visit
June 2010

Visitation times are the most challenging part of hospitalizations. For hours leading up to visitation, I feel uneasy. The shame of being hospitalized is coupled with intense feelings of loneliness. I limit visitations to my parents and closest friends.

With each visitation, my parents bring the familiar comfort of unconditional love and the ability to sit with me in the darkness. I long for the company to break up the day and lift my spirit. If I ask for anything, they are kind enough to bring it. Typically, it is outside food as a welcome break from the hospital buffet or a bag (or two or three) of my favorite candies.

I desperately miss my children and would do anything to spend time with them; I would also do just about anything to keep them from seeing me like this. After much internal deliberation, I decide it is probably best for Jordan and Micah to stay home. They shouldn't have to grow up with memories of visiting their mother in a psychiatric hospital.

When the kids came in the past, I ended up crying uncontrollably because I felt like a failure. The visits highlight that while I am in here, I cannot care for myself, let alone them. It pours salt on the soul-deep wounds.

I feel further removed from the outside world, but the isolation motivates me. I will do everything within my power to get discharged quickly.

Reverse Oregon Trail
July 2010

In the months following Aunt Gabrielle's death, there are changes and decisions to be made within the family. This all results in a rather sudden influx of family members. These people, who I barely remembered from the family reunion almost a decade ago, are now packing up and moving cross-country to our town. Not only our town, but some of them are also moving into my parents' house until they get settled. It is a packed house as the kids and I are also living there due to the foreclosure.

It's a reverse gold rush bringing people from the West to the Deep South. One of the travelers is Uncle Gary. Our relationship is practically starting from the ground up. Although Uncle Gary was present at the family reunion many years ago, his behavior was socially appropriate and, therefore, did not capture my attention. I was far more consumed with analyzing his younger brother, Uncle Greg. So now, I will have the privilege of getting to know Uncle Gary on a more personal level.

Truth be told, Uncle Gary may have been running from a few things and may have brought some troubles along; nevertheless, I quickly grow to admire him. We sit on the front porch and talk for hours. He smokes cigarettes, and we laugh. He tells hilarious stories and some hard truths. Perhaps because he has personally known some demons, he is equipped to handle mine.

It's a first for me. I am twenty-four years old and just now finding what it is like to have the support of extended family. I now have Uncle Gary - a family member I can relate to.

Over the next few months, Uncle Gary inevitably learns more about my deep depression. As we all bump shoulders squeezed into my parents' house, he sees me at my worst. He is there as I am repeatedly taken back to the psychiatric hospital. It doesn't seem to freak him out. He appears even-keeled, ready to listen, but also vulnerable enough to share a little about his own experiences. He tells me fragments of his story – his battles with depression.

Uncle Gary's deep, steady voice reminds me, "We are in this together. We are both going to do what it takes to get better."

{shock to the system}

New "Normal"
September 2010

I am terrified by the transformation that has occurred within my mind. Possibly even more concerning is that at other times, it isn't terrifying at all. I've come to accept this mental state as my new normal.

The pain is indescribable. I don't have much mental power to think of ways to ease this pain. I can only come up with one solution: suicide by any number of means.

I just want the pain to end. I need the pain to end. And the doctors just want me to be safe to keep going. After years of this struggle, maybe we can finally meet in the middle.

Electroconvulsive therapy (ECT) is a treatment option brought up as a last resort. It may seem like an extreme way to keep someone alive, but I will take some pretty drastic measures to make sure I die. Although I've only seen horrific depictions in an old movie, I'm in favor of the newly recommended treatment option.

Unbeknownst to me, several hospitals in the area perform ECT, including the psychiatric hospital I am currently admitted to. I can start just as soon as I've refrained from eating or drinking overnight.

Numb and hopeless, I take a short walk down the first-floor hallway to a room with cubbies. The staff advises me to place my belongings in a cubby and change into a gown. Everything, including the underwire bra, must go.

Now, I am ushered across the hall to the procedure room. It reminds me of a small emergency triage unit with five or six stretchers separated by curtains. The beds are arranged like rays of sunshine, with the head of the beds at the center of the room and the feet radiating out to the walls. Each partitioned area has a clock on the wall and a screen for monitoring vitals. The entire space feels sterile, with tile floors, artificial lighting, and a few stoic nurses. I will eventually come to recognize them.

The nurse guides me to an empty stretcher. Without hesitation, I climb into the crisp, white hospital sheets. The psychiatrist who will be doing the procedure strikes up a conversation, and we chat briefly. I don't remember the doctor explaining the risks of the procedure. I'm sure he did, but it doesn't matter anyway. The risks are the least of my worries. At this point, I will try anything for relief from the persistent depression if I can't do it my way.

The anesthesiologist rolls over on his stool, and the questions begin:

"When was the last time you had anything to eat or drink?" "Do you have any allergies?"

He starts my IV and begins the sedation process. I've spent enough time in hospitals to realize this all seems typical.

Across the room, I notice a cart with an open toolbox. It reminds me of something my Dad might have in his garage. They must use that for the seizure. My eyes are heavy, and I'm getting drowsy as the psychiatrist rolls the cart to the head of my bed.

The next thing I remember is opening my eyes. I don't move. I am still too tired for that. I can hear the staff talking over me. I hear the doctor's voice, "Hers lasted too long. We will have to turn it down next time." I don't say anything; I just listen.

70

While this may sound like an extremely frightening way to wake up, it isn't. All I can think about is the severe pain of depression. Nothing, not even a prolonged seizure, could be more frightening than my internal mental state.

Rinse & Repeat
(But ECT and Hospitalizations, Not Shampoo and Conditioner)
November 2010

The ECT treatments continue. I do some treatments on an outpatient basis; however, I am not stable enough to remain outpatient for long. I don't believe I can refrain from acting on the suicidal thoughts that torment my mind. As I'm readmitted to the adult unit, some of the staff members offer a kind, familiar greeting. They know me by name, a sure sign of a repeat failure. I feel like I know what the staff is thinking, "Leah, Frequent Flyer."

It is the same routine. The staff checks my bags, takes my vitals, and asks the same questions. Everything about the hospitalizations is the same, except for one thing – the unique mix of patients on the unit.

Discouraged and down, I don't plan to talk to anyone. Nevertheless, a guy approaches, asking, "Is this your first time?" He appears eager to share his newly acquired inpatient survival skills with me.

I slowly confess, "Um no, I've been here a lot of times."

His face displays his surprise as he blurts out, "You don't look like it."

I don't have the emotional energy to converse, but apparently, my outward appearance is not as disheveled as my inward state. With my head held low, I whisper, "Thank you."

The Third Degree
December 2010

Remaining inpatient for a planned week or two, I continue with ECT treatments on the same Monday, Wednesday, Friday schedule. I go about my morning in the typical fashion, sitting in group therapy sessions. When the staff is ready, I am pulled from the group and escorted to the floor where ECT is performed. The procedure runs smoothly and efficiently, finishing in under an hour.

Regardless of the degree of exhaustion, I always make a point to return to the group after the treatments. The nurses report on group participation, and the doctors take it as a good sign when a patient is attending groups, like getting your prison time reduced for good behavior.

Inescapably, it becomes public knowledge on the unit when someone is going for a procedure. There aren't many of us getting ECT treatments, so I get to be the center of the gossip. Not in a mean way. The other patients are just curious about ECT as they attempt to sort fact from fiction. They ask, "Does it hurt? Do you have a headache? Isn't it scary?" I diplomatically answer the numerous questions. "No, it didn't hurt. I don't have a headache. I don't think it's scary. I actually think it's starting to help."

Not Recording
January 2011

For whatever reason, I am unable to notice as bits of critical information subtly slip away. I concern myself with the essential tasks of eating, sleeping, and an occasional conversation. I move and process at a much slower rate. There are many changes I am unaware of and am frequently forgetting crucial information. What specifically am I forgetting? I don't even have enough self-awareness to know.

Regardless of what percentage of my impairment I am actually aware of, I do notice there seems to be an inverse relationship between the ECT treatments and my memory, particularly as the number of treatments reaches the upper teens and into the twenties.

I struggle to maintain long-term memories as well as retain new current information. It is like looking through the lens of a video camera. Everything appears clear and focused; however, one critical, small red dot is missing. The record button has malfunctioned. Information is processed through the lens of the mind but not retained. Details about what I've done over the day slip away.

Longer-term memories are also missing. I'm becoming increasingly frightened, as I can't recall things that undoubtedly happened. I look at my son, now three years old, and I don't remember being pregnant or having him. I don't know which hospital I gave birth in or how much he weighed. I don't know if he was a fussy baby or an easy baby. I don't remember him learning to walk, and I don't know his first words.

I know I am going through a divorce, but I don't remember meeting, getting engaged, having a wedding, or going on the Caribbean honeymoon. I am unsure when I decided to leave or anything about the police visit that led to a temporary restraining order against my ex. I know my house is in foreclosure, but I don't remember buying it or where I lived before.

After twenty-four sessions of ECT and the support of my family, I decide I am not able to continue the shock treatments. I will need another doctor and another treatment plan - a plan that doesn't leave me with a life I can't remember.

Fight For Freedom (to Drive)
January 2011

It has been three weeks since my last ECT treatment and even longer since I've had my driver's license. I have begged for it back at every doctor's visit. Are they really allowed to take my license? At today's visit, the psychiatrist and my parents finally agree to grant the return of my license, although none of them seem thrilled about the idea whatsoever. My extreme excitement quickly overshadows their apprehension.

Driving symbolizes the regaining of my independence. I don't have anywhere I need to go. I just want to be able to go if I desire. I don't like people telling me I can't do stuff. It feels repressive. The usurping of driving privileges was uncalled for, and I am confident I can drive just as well as I did pre-ECT. My parents drive me home with my new license in hand, but it will be the last time I need their help with transportation. I am now free to come and go as I please - free to live my independent, adult life.

After being home for only a short time, I feel the need to drive to get out of the house. I go to Wal-Mart. As I prepare to start the engine, it dawns on me. I can picture our street and the road in front of Wal-Mart, but I am missing all the connections in between. I mentally strain as I try to visualize what road comes after our street. After a few minutes of deep concentration, I can finally picture the turns I need to take. Thankfully there are only a few, and I succeed at my first post-ECT driving adventure.

Other trips are not as easy. I frequently print out directions from the computer (in the days of MapQuesting). I often call Dad and ask him how to get around town. It never occurred to me that I was missing this navigational ability until I began driving again. It also never occurs to me that this might be annoying to Dad. He frequently takes large chunks out of his day to verbally guide me over the phone as I drive (or more often than not, get lost).

With driving comes another realization about my cognitive impairments. My short-term memory is worse than I realized. I frequently continue to lose my car after I park. Not like a row or two off, but like, I have no idea in which direction to even begin walking. I learn to compensate by taking pictures of the location when I park the car, preferably by identifying landmarks such as cart returns or light posts. Parking garages are particularly helpful because they have letters and numbers posted throughout. When I walk out of the building, I pull out the photos in my phone for visual reminders for my car quest.

These impairments are disappointments and hindrances to my independence. I don't want to give up what little bit of freedom and normalcy I have left. I continue to drive, often lost and confused, but driving nonetheless.

Blank Stare
February 2011

How did I get here? What have I done in the past? How do I pick up where I left off if I don't remember? I have a recurring fear that I've hurt others' feelings without remembering. I mentally strain to bring forth memories that I know must be in there. Frustration sets in. It's no use. My memory is extremely limited.

Because of memorized facts, I know I grew up here, but still, it all feels so foreign. I study photographs in an attempt to call forth missing timeframes. I listen with curiosity and apprehension as others tell stories about my past. My mind struggles to piece together the fragments of my jumbled memory.

So many aspects of everyday life are new. I trust I've done these things, gone to these places, and experienced these situations before, yet I don't remember. My parents remind me that I used to know certain people. It just doesn't connect. I walk through the grocery store checkout; even the celebrities on the front of the magazines are foreign except for a few I remember from childhood.

As a child, my parents were strict – incredibly strict. There were plenty of PG movies we weren't allowed to watch, but "The Parent Trap" was allowed. I watched it over and over again. Now, I think of the twins' experiences as they have switched and gone to live with another parent they have only heard of but never known. I feel like a foreigner, an unfamiliar twin, in my own hometown.

I've heard rumors of these things. Unknown people keep recognizing me, and I think they must know my twin as I certainly don't remember or recognize them. I've heard these places exist. Supposedly I've been there many times; still, I can't picture the layout.

I try to memorize enough facts to cover the truth – I have very few recollections. I don't know how much memory is gone.

Professionals don't seem to focus on these types of deficits. They just continue asking about my mood.

Unforeseen Change Is in the Air
February 2011

Due to the severity of my symptoms, my new doctor, the professionals on my case, and my parents feel it would be best for me to see a counselor who specializes in what I have. I'm not sure exactly what that means. It is likely code that I've become more than most, including my old counselors, know what to do with me. I don't take it personally. They've given it their best but they don't know what to do with me either.

This new counselor, Dr. Simmons, wants me to work through a program of Dialectical Behavioral Therapy (DBT). Individual therapy is scheduled three days per week. I am not opposed if there is a chance it could work.

In our first session, Dr. Simmons lays out some ground rules, a crisis plan, and a no suicide contract. Wanting this process to work, I agree and sign the documents.

Dr. Simmons is different from other specialists. This one isn't afraid of the darkness. She is willing and wants to meet and coach me in the place where I am.

We spend very little time on the past and jump into the here and now. Mid-session, Dr. Simmons stops me. "What emotion are you feeling?"

Without hesitating, I reply, "Happy."

She tilts her head to the side a bit, her oversized earrings dangling, and asks, "Really? Your face doesn't look happy."

Of course, I am happy. Happy is the good thing to feel, it's what you're supposed to feel. As I think about the shape of my mouth, curving downward and my eyes attempting to barricade the pain and the tears that want to flow, it occurs to me that maybe I am not happy. The disconnect is unbelievable. This process is going to be a lot harder than I imagined.

I don't even know what I am feeling. I haven't allowed myself to feel, gosh, probably since my early elementary years. To stop feeling suicidal, I suppose I will have to start feeling and processing on a genuine level.

Dr. Simmons pulls out a feelings wheel. It is like a color wheel but with emotions instead of hues. I've never seen anything like this in my life. I realize I am emotionally illiterate with some incredibly intense feelings. Dr. Simmons talks about emotions in a way that makes me realize their power as indicators yet negates their ability to control.

Before I leave, Dr. Simmons gives me her phone number, a workbook, and a daily log. She genuinely wants me to call her when these overpowering thoughts appear, and not just as a liability concern. This is a profound and welcome change from the rigid plan of my previous doctors. Suicidal ideations always warranted calling the doctor, who always just said "get to the hospital." But now, Dr. Simmons and I are supposed to work through the dysregulation together with as few hospitalizations as possible.

Will this even work? What do I have to lose? Not much. What could I possibly gain? I guess something. Right now, I am not able to make it in the outside world. I've lost all faith in my ability to handle the ups and downs of everyday life. Unless I want to live most of my life in the psychiatric hospital, I need a drastic change. My current track record is unsustainable and less than mediocre. Here goes nothin'.

A Tired Like Nothing I've Ever Experienced Before
March 2011

The combination of psychiatric medications is causing me to sleep excessively. I wake up feeling just as tired as when I went to sleep. The exhaustion is comparable to a severe flu. I am fatigued from walking around the house or playing with the children even for a few minutes. I struggle to carry out daily activities I once did with ease.

I think back to the productive years of the past, the times when my work ethic showed. As a little kid, I worked hard for chore money. As a teenager, I babysat most nights of the week and even through nursing school. I recall the long hours that I put in at the hospital. That is all gone. What is left is a shell of a person. I am nothing more than a sedated, near zombie-like figure. I've boiled down to the most primitive experience - my life is made up of little more than eating and sleeping.

I am not eating kale and tofu, far from it. The more exhausted I am, the more I crave sugar. It's a pathetic cry for any type of pick-me-up. Food cravings inundate my day; this time, it's for brownies. I pull out the mixing bowl and the ingredients, placing them down on my parents' kitchen counter.

It's slightly encouraging that I even feel up to baking something. I read the instructions on the box of brownies. Wait what? For some reason, the directions (all four steps) seem more confusing than they used to. I reread the instructions, which are too much to keep straight. I focus on the first step. I snip the corner of the mix and dump it in the mixing bowl. Slowly and methodically, I reread the second step pausing to comprehend. I follow the instructions, tossing in the ingredients. Back to the box. What is next? I stare at the box and freeze. I have no idea what steps I have completed. Have I done oil? Have I done the egg?

I do not have any recollection of following any steps. There are three ingredients to add, and it is too challenging. I peer over the mixing bowl and stare at the indiscernible amount of contents. Time passes. I continue to stare. Eventually, I detect an egg amidst the chocolate powder. I haven't stirred anything, and the yolk is sitting on top. I start again from the egg step. I don't know if this is right or wrong, and I don't understand why it is so hard. Aside from driving, this is my first clue that my mind has changed, and life will be a lot harder.

That same individual who thrived on "adulting" and took pride in being independent now needs help with just about everything. At this point, it isn't clear what would be salvageable and what would be gone for good. Crumbling under the jurisdiction of mental illness and the disappointment of current medical treatment, hope continues to slip away.

Blank Check
March 2011

I attempt to pay a bill. I hold the pen in my right hand as I stare at my checkbook. The pages are spread open to a blank check, but what do I write? I have been mailing checks for years, but now I can't process how to fill them out. I stare and wait, hoping it will come to me. This is not the case.

Finally, Mom points to the top line and says, "This is for who it is to." This newly-tedious process continues with her guidance, line by line until I fill out the check. Not only is money tight to pay the bills, but I also can't even figure out step one - how to write a check on my own. This is a far cry from where I used to be.

I've spent enough time in hospitals and caring for the elderly that I have my own preconceived notions about the presentation of memory loss. I imagine a sweet person with thinning or nonexistent hair in their late 80's, maybe even early 90's, asking, "Honey, where am I? How'd I get here? What year is it?" At twenty-four years old, I never imagined that I would be asking similar questions. I try my best to hide how confused I am and what I've forgotten.

Losing memories is different from other medical issues I've had in the past. Once, my dog jumped up and hit my nose. I cried but went along with life. Later on, I had an X-ray for sinus issues, and the doctor informed me that I had suffered a broken nose in the past. Cut and dry.

It's quite a bit different with memories. What do I do? Go to the doctor and say, "I'm missing a bunch of memories, huge chunks of my life. The thing is, I can't tell you what memories are gone because I don't know. And you don't know what memories because they weren't yours to begin with."

Memories are also tricky because there is a school of thought that some will come back over time. Which ones? Over how much time?

A Selective Inventory of Memories
March 2011

As I sit in a chair in Dr. Simmons's office, I complain about my memory loss. The more aware I become, the more I realize how bad it truly is. She asks about the memories that remain. I can recall things from childhood; while not as vivid, some are still there. Dr. Simmons reminds me that the fading of memories with time is normal, and many people don't have many childhood memories. I agree. I am not too worried about my childhood memories. I am concerned about NOW. I am concerned about the last seven or eight years of my life that are missing.

As I verbalize all of my memories from adulthood, I come up with remarkably few, astonishingly less than I had assumed I had. Dr. Simmons points out that I don't have any positive memories. It's true. The only memories from adulthood are emotionally-charged, traumatic, and frightening. It's as if my mind is limited to "Breaking News."

Dr. Simmons asks, "How do you think this impacts your view of the world?" This question sparks a groundbreaking revelation. It is no wonder the world feels like a frightening and depressing place.

I don't want this to be my truth. This insight begins my search for the positive. I will do all I can to find evidence of the good that was and remains in the world. If the old memories won't come back, I will have to make positive new ones and hold onto them.

God Hates Me
March 2011

It is one thing to believe in God or a Higher Power when all is going well. It's another thing to try to trust when it seems that you are doomed. Why pray when your prayers seem to fall on deaf ears? Why go to church when everyone else seems happy? This season is not joyful. It's not even a season that can be faked - my disheveled appearance, slowed speech, forgetful mind, and tearful eyes scream, "I'm a hot mess!"

Why would a caring, supernatural being allow its "treasured child" to go through this? I can't bear to watch my kids cry after a scraped knee, and I'm not even God. God should know better. I know this isn't the case for everyone, but my faith dwindles with every hurdle, every letdown, and every indication that there is no hope for the future. And then I beat myself up for my lack of faith.

Every once in a while, I go to church (purposefully late to sit in the back row and sneak out early). Attending church is a struggle for many reasons. I've been a member of this church for ten years. These people surrounded me and loved me through a teen pregnancy. Now, it feels like too much to honestly share all of the recent losses. Maybe I could tell just one downplayed loss, such as the marriage didn't work out, I'm not at that job anymore, or my dream house ended up in foreclosure, or I've been feeling a little down lately. There is no way to tell it all, but neither is there a way to fake it all.

Another reason church is a struggle is that memory loss has wiped out all of the Bible stories I learned. I purposefully don't bring my Bible because I have forgotten everything in it, even the names of the books of the Bible. If Pastor asks us to turn to a particular verse, it will be much less noticeable if I *Oops, forgot my Bible* as I was running out the door than if I can't even figure out what direction to begin flipping.

But most of all, I am terrified someone will ask, "How are you?" This dread is the exact reason I must leave while Pastor is still preaching. I will surely burst into tears if anyone asks. I can't even muster up a fake smile or the word "fine." I want to answer the question, "How are you?" with the honest answer, "Cursed! I believe God takes pleasure in making my life miserable." How does one share that? Even the mention of 'God' makes me sob.

Giving the honest answer to social greetings is generally frowned upon, so I run from the question and the people who ask it.

Then one day, it happens - the unavoidable. A lady I've known on an acquaintance level for years walks up and asks the dreaded question, "How are you?" As I knew I would, I burst into tears. I sob too hard to explain. Too hard to even begin to apologize, but she just draws me in. I cry and cry, and cry - snotty-nosed, out-of-breath textbook "ugly crying." She doesn't ask questions or try to say it will all be okay. She just wraps her arms around me and holds me for as long as the tears fall.

The pain is still there after the experience, only slightly more tolerable. I didn't feel so alone in the struggle, and when my most dreaded moment happened, it was okay. More than okay. For those few minutes, I was authentic. As she held me, I felt that she was bearing my burden with me

Every once in a while, I see her around but I still don't know her well. I'm pretty sure she never knew the full extent of my pain, yet she made it better by embracing me in my sorrow.

I wish I could have whispered insight to myself at this point. *Leah, this is going to be a long, hard process. Quit resisting.* I was so focused on getting back into the workforce that I bordered on the edge of denial. I wanted lightning-fast therapy and instant pills to get a new job. I didn't want the losses to be true.

I didn't want to be a "taker." I'd been a worker and a "giver" all of my life. But what this young version of me didn't know was that this genuinely was a "taking" season. It's okay to have these seasons, just as it's okay to have giving seasons. You just have to know when the season is right for each of these and when it's time to switch. I would look at that broken shell of a young lady in her big, brown eyes and say, "You will not be a "taker" forever. You have a bright future that will require a while to get to, longer than you want, but I promise, you will have something to give."

{picking up pieces of life}

An Example of How to Bomb an Interview
March 2011

At this point, it's been months without a job, without a purpose in life or a structured reason to get dressed in the morning. I realize the first step to securing a job requires filling out an application, so I practice reciting my birthday and address. They come back relatively quickly. My social security number is much more challenging, so I continue to practice.

I read nursing books, but I forget what I've read. Sometimes, I will come across a medical term and think, *Oh, Oh! I've heard that before! But I realize I don't know what it means.* I worked incredibly hard to become a nurse, and now it's - poof - gone.

Over time, I get teeny bits and pieces of nursing knowledge back, yet not enough to comprise any marketable skills. There is no way I could go back to the profession. I don't even remember what the college campus looked like or the names of any of my professors. I certainly don't know enough about the medications, diseases, procedures, etc., to safely get back to work. I sob once more over what I've lost and, ultimately, who I've become.

While painstakingly researching for job possibilities, I see an advertisement for a company that needs monitor technicians. I can do this. I used to read heart monitors all shift long when I worked in the cardiac care unit. Being a monitor technician could be the solution. It is a tiny percentage of nursing. I could relearn that part and have a job.

I am excited about the opportunity and pull out an old workbook on interpreting heart rhythms. I can't find my old calipers to measure the waves, so I buy new ones. As I open the EKG book, my heart sinks. It is like a foreign language. I know I have heard some of these words before, but I have no recollection of what they mean. I might not be starting from square one, but it is pretty close.

All of the confidence I had quickly fades. I will have to try to teach myself this entire EKG book before the interview. I study numerous hours a day.

After a week of studying what I thought I already knew, it is time for the interview. I compartmentalize my feelings of inadequacy and instability as I approach the building. *Stand tall. Look confident. Don't let anyone find out how crazy you are.*

An employee kindly greets me and begins sharing about the company. The heart rhythms are transmitted here, where they are monitored and interpreted for changes. An EMT applying for a second job joins us on the tour. As the employee leads us around the facility, I see people attentively watching many screens in cubicles.

The tour wraps up as we loop around to the front of the building. The employee states, "As part of the interview, we need you both to read some strips."

I am nervous yet confident. The ad mentioned reading strips, and I've been practicing nearly nonstop.

I sit down next to the EMT. The employee hands each of us a thick packet of heart rhythms to interpret, reassuring us that it is okay to take our time.

I thumb through the pages. I hardly remember anything of what I've studied this past week. I have nothing left from nursing school. I stare. I panic as a tear drops down my cheek. *Oh, no, Leah, not now. Not at a job interview. She will know you are unstable, and this is your only chance. Pull it together.* I have no way of disguising my tears or my feelings of incompetency.

Frantically I say, "I'm sorry, I have to go." I hurry out the front door, leaving the other candidate as he continues writing answers. Concerned, the interviewer follows me out to the sidewalk. She tries to explain that it is okay. Between sobs, I fumble for words, "I've been sick for a really long time. I thought it was time to come back to work, but I don't think so."

She pats me on the shoulder, saying some reassuring words that don't even register. I am thinking of ways to escape the embarrassment and reality of my vocational loss.

Abraham Lincoln Was The First President
March 2011

It is becoming increasingly clear that I'm not capable of working, definitely, not in the same capacity as I used to. Every day I pray I will get my memory back and return to life as I knew it. If I could just remember, maybe I could work.

All of the practicing and praying in the world isn't enough.

Dad and I (mostly Dad) fill out the disability paperwork. There doesn't seem to be any other option. I'm flat broke, in the hole, and the house is gone. I am paying $664/month for COBRA to extend my health insurance. Dad explains the limitations; I am running out of time yet can't afford to go without it.

A little while after mailing the disability forms and my medical records, I get a notice requiring me to meet with a government-appointed psychiatrist. I follow through.

He is in an office located about fifteen minutes from my house. It is in a small building resembling a townhouse. As I walk in for my appointment, I'm unsure how this process works. I've only heard horror stories of people not getting approved when they most needed it.

Leah, just do your best.

Deep down, I am torn between realizing my dire financial situation and wanting with every fiber of my being to be alright and capable of working.

The doctor invites me to sit. He implies that he sees his own clients and does these disability evaluations on the side. He inquires about what I did for work.

"I was a registered nurse."

The psychiatrist asks about my diagnosis and why I can't work anymore.

I explain, "I have bipolar, and the ECT treatments messed up my memory."

He keeps a straight face. I can't tell if he believes me or not. He asks about any addictions.

I share that I drank as a wild teenager and did some things, but not anymore.

He asks, "What was your favorite type of alcohol?"

"I didn't have one."

He shares that his daughter is an alcoholic and only likes a specific brand of vodka. I don't know why he is sharing this, but oddly enough, it eases the butterflies in my stomach. I suppose it is the comfort of knowing the evaluator and his family aren't perfect either.

The psychiatrist continues to ask a series of questions. Some are easy, and others are tough. I am proud of myself when I know the answer and can blurt it out quickly. I feel as if I am on a game show - winning points for correct answers.

He requests, "Tell me the names of four presidents."

I am stumped. Trying to play it off, I counter with, "I'm not into politics." I don't even know who the president is right now.

He encourages, "Just try. Who was the first president?"

I blurt out, "Abraham Lincoln."

He chuckles, "Kids these days."

We continue on to more questions; it feels like hours before they are finally done. I don't remember any more of them, but I am confident I did well.

The psychiatrist explains he will complete a report for the disability office, and I will hear from them regarding the decision/outcome.

Recording in Three, Two, One
April 2011

I can't pinpoint when it started happening, but miraculously, I seem to be retaining new memories. The "record button" is functioning again. Hallelujah.

Before, I didn't notice memories were drifting away. Maybe I went to bed with them and forgot them by morning? Perhaps they slipped away unannounced throughout the day?

But now, something has changed.

New memories are beginning to stick instead of slipping away into the abyss of forgetfulness. I remember what happened yesterday, and I recall what occurred a week ago. This is good.

However, I realize the new capability has not restored the past. Memories from years leading up to ECT and the first few months following the treatment remain absent.

I focus less on figuring out what is gone and more on finding ways to conceal the deficits. I only wish to be normal again.

The Far-Reaching Arms of Mental Illness
April 2011

For the first time, I am beginning to realize what I've put others through. It wasn't something I noticed. But now, it is becoming evident. I see the soul-level fatigue in my parents' eyes. It is the type of exhaustion my parents can't fix with a nap or even a vacation. Dad and Mom look like they would cry if they could, but they ran out of tears a long time ago.

I don't have enough courage to ask them how they are coping. I'm afraid of the truth, afraid to hear of the immeasurable amount of pain I've inflicted despite good intentions.

I also know the instability must be hard on the kids. Because I feel helpless, I also avoid asking the kids how they are handling it all. I fear I know the answer - not well at all. Jordan has been sent to the principal's office fourteen times this year. He'd never been before. Micah now expresses his toddler-sized emotions through tantrums and rage instead of words. The more dysregulated I become, the more my children's behavior declines, and I feel more helpless. The behaviors become cyclical. As much as I long for stability and normalcy, I don't know how to achieve it.

Bipolar has wreaked havoc not only on me but everyone around me.

Fresh Eyes
April 2011

Perhaps the ECT helped keep me alive, sustaining me in a way nothing else could have, through a dreadfully dark place; however, ECT didn't cure me by any stretch of the imagination. I work feverishly to attain stability. I attend counseling sessions and fill out emotion-regulation worksheets like a full-time job. However, I continue to struggle with my emotions and moods on a daily basis.

I wish someone would have warned me that it is possible to do everything right with bipolar (therapy, medication compliance, sleep regulation, and self-care) and STILL have mood changes or even suicidal thoughts.

Today, my thoughts are frightening and, again, centered around ending the pain for no particular reason. For the first time since working with Dr. Simmons, she is recommending hospitalization, as I am not stable enough to continue our work at this time. Hospitalization feels like a failure after experiencing a tiny glimpse of stability.

Due to insurance changes, I am taken to another hospital with a new treatment team and a fresh perspective.

Razors Are a Delicacy
April 2011

After eight days in the hospital, I wish I'd brought more clothes! I make do pairing the same yoga pants and gray hoodie with a few different tank tops. I glance down at the empty grommets on my jacket hood where the drawstring used to be. I am reminded of how small my world is. Freedoms I used to take for granted have been usurped, yet again.

I didn't bother to bring any makeup, only lip balm for the dry hospital air. I am not allowed a hairdryer, so I toss my frizzy, air-dried hair into a messy bun. I don't have the energy for primping anyway.

What I miss more than I'd ever imagined is shaving my legs! The prickles that have been growing over the past week remind me that I can't be trusted with anything, certainly not razors. I don't have a personal history of cutting or violence; it's just a general blanket rule for all the patients, like the no-string rule.

It's hard to feel optimistic and comfortable in your skin with dirty clothes and wooly legs. I can get over re-wearing clothes, but hairy legs have become one of the most distressing parts of hospitalization.

Fed up and becoming slightly frantic, I approach my nurse begging, "Can I please shave my legs? It's been a week and I can't take it anymore. I'm not a cutter. I don't even care if someone watches. I need to shave my legs."

I honestly expect a cold rejection, but to my surprise, she replies, "Let me finish this, and then I'll come."

A short while later, the nurse enters the room with a cheap, blue hospital razor. I don't care that the head of the razor doesn't twist with the contours of the leg or that it doesn't have multiple blades for the closest shave. I'm relieved that I finally get to shave and feel clean again.

The nurse stands outside the bathroom door with a distance that feels comfortable considering the circumstances - giving privacy while ensuring my safety.

I repeatedly thank her for her time. I return the razor through the partially drawn shower curtain, and she leaves me to finish my shower.

They say it's the little things in life. Shaving my legs is one of those small things - an act of kindness that will stand out as one of the most compassionate moments of my hospitalizations. As I run my fingers over my smooth legs, there is a sense of relief.

You Don't Belong Here
April 2011

A staff member of the psychiatric hospital pulls together three chairs at the end of a hallway, starting an impromptu small group session. He invites Lexie, another patient, and me to join.

In a professional manner, he asks, "What brought you here? What's your story?"

Lexie shares about her bipolar, struggles at work, and the devastating loss of a baby - all have contributed to her downward spiral. I tell about my drawn-out divorce, the bipolar diagnosis, and the many hospitalizations (now in the double digits).

After listening and talking with us for close to an hour, he looks at me and utters, "I've worked here for many years. I've seen a lot of patients. You don't belong here. I mean, we are always here if you need us, but you don't belong here."

I remain outwardly calm and pretend to be attentive to the conversation's conclusion. Inwardly, I am screaming *WHAT? How do I NOT belong in the psychiatric hospital? I'm a frequent flier. I am crazy as can be!*

Somewhere along the way, without even noticing, I have shifted from feeling like I must get back to my life, as I certainly don't belong in the mental institute, to internalizing the label of a frequent flier, psychiatric patient. Being a psychiatric patient has intertwined with my deepest sense of identity, and I can't imagine anything different for myself.

The psychiatric hospital is the only place I know how to function. The bar is set at a relatively low level, and I can't possibly meet any higher expectations. I can sit in a chair in a group, eat in a cafeteria, stay out of fights, and be kind to the staff, but that is about it. Functioning outside of the hospital requires stamina, stability in the face of challenges, and mental acuity I simply do not have.

How do I NOT fit in here? I am confused, slightly offended, and even scared.

As I process, replaying his words, I realize this is scary but scary in a good way. This is the first time a mental health professional has told me of my potential. This conversation is a monumental occasion that marks a significant paradigm shift in my thinking. I begin to feel slightly empowered. Someone believes my future can look different than my past.

Friends Since... I Can't Remember
April 2011

I see Camila, my best friend, quite a bit. She calls on an almost-daily basis and stops by often, whether that be in the hospital or at my place. I don't know where she came from or how we met. I just know it was at some point during the ECT fog. And now she is just here.

Superficial friends, the ones who might otherwise take a lifetime to weed out, have been eliminated almost instantly with the occurrence of mood swings and memory loss. They've quit returning my calls or have found elaborate ways to avoid me. It is excruciating to watch long-standing relationships come to an end so quickly.

It is fair to say that I have been a lot to deal with through these last stages of life and treatment, only I didn't realize it. I work hard to make sure that conversations with friends are a two-way deal. I am not calling these people just to complain for hours. I try to be optimistic. I minimize how dark the darkness truly is in an attempt to protect my friends' hearts. I have been to some horrific emotional places, and I would never want to drag them (or anyone for that matter) down. So, I believe I'm a "good friend." What I don't realize is how memory loss impacts friendships.

It is at this point, now that the ECT-related fog has started to clear and my mental camera is recording, that Camila has the heart to share a little. She does it in her typical gentle and gracious way. Camila knows me well and knows it will sting; that's why she has held off this long.

Camila starts by reminding me of how well I am doing and how far I've come - emphasizing my progress.

And then she begins to tenderly share about a conversation we've had... or really multiple conversations about the same topic.

On a random weekday, Camila had mentioned that her daughter would be going for a doctor's appointment the following day. Knowing I would need a reminder, I wrote a note to check on the appointment, which I did: each and every day. Sometimes numerous times in the same day.

I don't recall any of this, but Camila states I called to check on that appointment repeatedly. Camila would share how it went, acting as if it were the first time we'd had this conversation. Not only did I forget Camila's report of the appointment, but I also forgot to throw away the post-it note reminder after she informed me how it went.

Like only the kindest of friends would do, Camila was gracious enough to protect me, never telling me that we already talked about this today. And yesterday. And for days before that. She knew I was too fragile and destitute to handle the truth.

100

It was like a Bill Murray type "Groundhog Day" with the kindest of the kind. Camila deserves an award. She knew that this was my best, me trying to be a thoughtful friend.

Not everybody could understand or make time for that.

At this moment, I understand how much I honestly was to deal with. I cry a bit, and I thank Camila for her friendship. And cry a bit more.

However, losing some of the more frivolous relationships is a silver lining as I am now left with an amazing (although smaller) core group of incredibly supportive friends.

Camila is one of about six or seven friends who have swooped in tighter the more challenging life has gotten. Hoping to lift my mood, this group of genuine friends got together and wrote things they liked about me on pieces of scrapbook paper and placed them in a large jar. Every day I get to pull out an encouraging word or affirmation. (On bad days, I cheat and pull out two. It's alright. They put a ton in there.)

These are the people who won't settle for blatantly false "happy answers." These friends don't need me to filter my language or want me to downplay the severity of my pain. They willingly enter the alternate universe, the psychiatric hospital in which I spend a significant amount of time. They show up at visitation hours when I am at my lowest, even if they have just worked a full day and have a family waiting at home. These are the friends who will supportively listen at all hours, even if I make the call from the mental institute. They visit me at home between hospital admissions. These are absolutely no-matter-what friends.

Chatter on the Bleachers
(The Beginning of What Would Be an Eight Year Romantic
Relationship and Lifelong Friendship)
April 2011

My energy levels are starting to increase. I feel far from my old self, but I welcome even the most minor positive changes. I still need occasional help with the kids, although nothing compared to before.

On one of those occasions where I needed a break, Dad took Jordan to the local skate park, and, ever since, Jordan has been obsessed. Having a child pick up skateboarding sounds terrific, except the skate park has one specific rule - children cannot be left unattended until age eleven. Jordan is eight. Sitting on the bleachers overseeing his safety consumes my unemployed days.

There is, however, one perk - the attractive worker at the entrance. I see him frequently but never actually speak to him. He has a bit of a babyface, so I struggle to guess his age. I glance over at him on occasion while reminding myself I'm in no condition to even think about dating.

Out of sheer boredom, I finally interrupt his deep train of thought. "What are you reading?"

He closes his book, gets up from his chair, climbs the bleachers, and sits down beside me. It was almost as if he was waiting for me to give a signal that it was acceptable to approach. Like me, he is tired of watching the same kids trying the same stunts for the hundredth time. Tricks with names that sound like gibberish. We both have to be here; we might as well talk.

It turns out that "Babyface" has a name - Tommy. After a few minutes of talking, I get the feeling he is a little confused by me. He shares, "I've been trying to figure out if you're Jordan's babysitter or his parent."

I divulge, in the most classy way I can concoct, that I've been through quite a bit. The kid skating out there is indeed my son. I had him at sixteen. That isn't enough to evoke any outward sign of shock. I planned to scare Tommy away on the front end to avoid future disappointment for myself, but he's still listening. So I continue with the fact that I married a controlling and manipulative man who does everything he can to make my life miserable. I share about my ex-husband's attempts to smoke me out and then force me to return to him. Still more, weaving in the fact that I've been diagnosed with bipolar, requiring shock treatments which have messed up my memory. I emphasize how unfit I am to date with each piece of my story. I tell him about my current situation - that I can't work and have resorted to living at home with my parents.

It's a lot, way more than I would usually squeeze into any conversation, but I don't want him to get any ideas. I just word vomited my crazy life in one sitting.

For some bizarre reason, Tommy remains seated and engaged in our conversation. He tells me about himself and his previous failed relationship and dropping out of college. Time flies, and before I know it, we've talked until closing time. Three hours have passed.

Black Box Warnings
May 2011

Previously, other doctors have increased dosages and added medications at any hint of mood instability. This psychiatrist is different. Dr. Morris seems to have an innovative perspective. She vows to avoid entire classes of drugs I was on during the frequent suicide attempts, citing literature and black box warnings.

Instead of increasing medications until I'm vacantly drooling in a corner, she calculates carefully and lowers the dose. Even with severe symptoms, I seem to respond better to a small, child-sized amount. Lowering dosages seems so counterintuitive, yet it seems to be working a bit.

To-Do List: Stay Around
May 2011

It's a close call and a hard decision, but I have decided I want to stay around for a while. The good in life does outweigh the bad. It is likely a combination of many factors, including the medications starting to work, what I'm learning in therapy with Dr. Simmons, my mood creeping upward, and the sunshine of spring, but I want to make it out of this victorious. My mentality has shifted from ending the pain to working through it. Huge.

For months and months, I have been promising doctors, psychologists, and caseworkers that I will be safe (most of it intentionally misleading to get discharged). Honestly, I am not sure the psychiatric hospital is the best environment for finding one's will to survive, but it has kept me safe long enough for some type of change to occur.

Crap. Now, there is a new challenge. If I try to stay alive, I have the daunting task of reintegrating into society. I am going to have to try to be normal. It is a foreign concept that I don't know how to begin practicing. I don't want to be noticeable because being noticeable means risking exposure as mentally ill.

There are so many reasons this isn't going to work. I can carry on a conversation as long as it relates to the present, as in today and this exact moment.

However, I still don't remember much about my children or myself. During conversations, I give a minimal number of vague responses. It is hard to chat when you don't know what you have forgotten about the other person. I am often uncertain of my history with others, where I know them from, let alone any details about their lives. Sometimes I'm not even lucky enough to get the 'I know you from somewhere but can't put my finger on it' feeling. I stick with vague questions. "How have you been?" and "What's new?" are safe conversation starters and help maintain the pretense of normalcy.

From there, the topic of politics is an exposure waiting to happen. I have forgotten everything about the government. I hear mention of significant events such as September 11th and Katrina, but I haven't the faintest recollection of them. Entertainment is out of the question if I am going to integrate into society. I have forgotten all but a few movies I have ever seen. I've also forgotten famous actors and musicians. Sometimes, I surprise myself as the words to songs come back to me (music seems easier to recall), but that's about it.

Trying to be normal is exhausting but a worthy pursuit.

Sparks Fly and Questions Arise
May 2011

I just so happen to show up at the skatepark on days when Tommy is working. His company is one of the highlights of my week.

As we sit on the bleachers, I struggle to make conversation.

Tommy asks, "Tell me more about what you like to do?"

"Jordan plays flag football and Micah likes dinosaurs."

Tommy probes, "Yes, but I want to know about you. You do this a lot - answer everything I ask about you with something about your kids."

What! How dare he say that? If he is going to like me, he will have to like my kids, too.

I realize Tommy's comment has nothing to do with liking my kids. It has to do with knowing me separately from my children, and I have no separately.

Oh crap! Who am I outside of my kids?

Sensing my panic, he explains, "I'm not mad. I really like you. I think you had to grow up quickly and never got the chance to figure out who you are."

I fumble for the words, "I don't really know who I am outside of my kids."

This process is going to be interesting, taking time and patience on both of our parts as I learn to grow into my own skin. But the new challenge sparks some excitement.

Walking Meditation
June 2011

I've joined Dr. Simmons's DBT group in addition to my regular individual sessions. Today our group is doing a surprise outing, a much-welcomed change. We leave our bags and workbooks as we walk out of the office space and across the street. There stands a breathtaking, large historic church with intricate stonework and gothic-style arches. Dr. Simmons leads us down a sidewalk and around the back of the campus to an open grass area. There, in the middle, lies a labyrinth composed of bricks flush with the ground. Dr. Simmons describes the ancient spiritual tradition of meditating while slowly walking a labyrinth.

It sounds a little fishy, and I'm not feeling the vibe. I allow the other group members to go ahead of me. Wanting to comply with Dr. Simmons's wishes, I place one foot on a brick. The grass peeks up between the cracks - heel to toe, heel to toe. I slowly begin to walk the path. As soon as I've made it a few steps, the course changes direction, seemingly back toward where I started. A few more steps and another sharp turn.

My focus begins to deepen as the other group members fade out of consciousness. I am overwhelmed with an intense revelation, likely the point of the entire exercise. Life feels like a cruel labyrinth with numerous twists and turns. I don't feel like I am getting anywhere or making any progress. I fight to hold back the tears that are welling up. I continue walking in the same slow heel-toe fashion. "One step at a time." and "One foot in front of the other." It is now clear I have only one duty - continue walking and trust the path, regardless of the twists and turns.

A Jab Right in the Heart, Cancel That, the Boob
August 2011

The strangest thing happened. In the middle of a conversation about who knows what, Dad made a quick joke, a little jab, about getting "touched up." He was looking directly at me when he said it.

I chuckled to hide the confusion. I have no idea what Dad is talking about. I've never had surgery. My mind gets the vaguest portion of a memory. Questions speed through my head. *Wait, did I get plastic surgery? A boob job? Oh my gosh. Maybe I did. I can't believe these aren't mine. When did I get them done?*

I don't know the answers to the questions, and I sure don't want to ask my Dad. That would be even more awkward than his "joke."

I wait until I'm alone in my bedroom to take my shirt off and search for scars. Sure enough, I see a faint line under each breast. *I did get them touched up.* I try to remember the details but am unable. I can't remember anything about the doctor, where I had it done, or the recovery period. All that comes back is a vague memory of having the procedure right after breastfeeding Micah so no one would notice the difference.

This realization frightens me. I have forgotten my history. *If I forgot about breast augmentation, what else did I forget? I could have lost a kidney to the black market without ever knowing.*

I continue removing my clothes, searching for more scars. I notice six tiny marks on my abdomen with a large vertical scar below my belly button. As I think back for a while, I am eventually able to recall I had my gallbladder and appendix out. They weren't at the same time. I don't know which came first. I don't know why, what doctors, or what hospitals. As I study the unusual vertical scar, I picture a doctor's face and his lips saying, "We didn't know we were going to have to take out your appendix when we were doing the exploratory surgery. The incisions were already in other places, so we had to take your appendix out through your belly button." I am relieved that I solved enough of the mystery of my abdominal incisions to have a vague understanding of what happened.

The last scar I find is a jagged u-shaped scar, which encircles a knuckle on my right hand. I study the incision. Based upon interpreting the scar pattern through my spotty nursing memories, it seems like there were stitches at some point. I rack my brain, but nothing comes to mind.

Eventually, I give up and call Mom to randomly ask, "Do you know how I got this scar on my knuckle?"

She says, "Yes, you cut it on a glass vase at your house and had to go to the emergency room for stitches."

I pause. I was hoping Mom's explanation would give me something to pull from, but I still have no recollection of that. Having no reason whatsoever to doubt her, I respond with a puzzled yet accepting "Hum, okay."

It is a feeling like nothing else I've ever known. I am here, at this moment in this place, and for the most part, I don't know how I've gotten here.

Each Pill: Let Down or Hope
August 2011

Medications are still being adjusted. No one warned me that psychiatric medications aren't like other drugs. For example, I've had strep throat many times, and the treatment is simple; an antibiotic that the strain will respond to, and within a day or two, I'm feeling significantly better.

My experience with psychiatric medications has been drastically different. After more than twenty medication combinations, we're still learning.

It's relatively common to wait a few weeks before any possibility of improvement can be detected. With signs of improvement often come side effects. Daily doses of Benadryl have been part of the regiment, crucial to diminish involuntary facial movements. I've had combinations that seem promising until something, such as a life-threatening rash, necessitates the immediate discontinuation of the drug. At other times, I've been so medicated that I feel physically numb in a dreamy reality.

I wasn't prepared for how many times I would be let down; however, each new medication comes with the hope of a brighter, more stable future. I cross my fingers and nonchalantly pray to the same God who torments me.

Nocturnal Apartment Hunting
August 2011

I'd sincerely hoped the most recent hospitalization would be my last. That is not the case. The doctor requires another admission to supervise a risky medication change and admits me for a short observation period.

I'm not thrilled about being away, but this hospitalization is difficult for a more pressing reason. My relationship with Dad and Mom is strained. We love each other dearly, yet clearly should not live together. That whole 'parenting while being parented' dynamic that emerged when I was sixteen with little Jordan has reared its ugly head and is back. My parents are not thrilled with how I care for my children in often sedated states with irritable moods. I'm not thrilled with how they micromanage my best shot at parenting.

I need space with my children to fight this as a nuclear family. I need somewhere else to go when I leave the hospital.

I share the dilemma with the caseworker. I tell the nurses about the need for housing. It seems useless, and my frustration builds. I desperately need an apartment and cannot search for one because I'm stuck in the psychiatric hospital. I need Internet access to research rent prices. I'd feel so much better if I could get a list of phone numbers to call regarding availability. I'm left without options, forced to wait idly without access to any resources.

While the ECT and incredibly strong medications have subdued many facets of my personality, the go-getter aspect has not been. Barriers to forward progress, including this situation, are infuriating.

111

In the evening, my nurse calls me to the medication room. She hands me a small paper cup full of various pills and a slightly larger cup of water. I throw back all the pills, and they are down in one swallow. The nurse checks for pocketing - in my cheeks or under my tongue. I'm done and free to go.

She leans in closer and whispers, "Come back to the nurse's station once the other patients are in bed. I'll let you use my computer to look for apartments."

I let out a deep sigh of relief and thank her repeatedly. I feel validated and seen as not only a dime-a-dozen patient but as a human being. This act of kindness, like others along the way, will continue to stand out for years to come.

I do find a place. The nocturnal internet search from the nurses' station proves successful. I'll be moving in within the week. This will be the first time I've been on my own in over a year, and the thought of regaining my treasured independence thrills me.

Open House, Open Mind
September 2011

It is easy to get so caught up in managing my own symptoms that I forget about the variables in the surrounding environment. I automatically assume something is wrong with me, overlooking that my symptoms don't occur in an isolated bubble. Some of the madness isn't related to my bipolar at all - it's just life, but it can be hard to differentiate.

I am the most self-aware of my deficits (aware of my shortcomings and what others seem to have) when I go to Jordan's school. The carpool line serves as a scheduled reminder of my inferiority. At 8:35 a.m. and 3:35 p.m., five days a week, I am surrounded by perfectly put-together mothers giggling on their phones while they wait in their expensive SUVs.

Today is particularly challenging - Open House at Jordan's elementary school.

I sit in the car, attempting to prepare mentally. I feel like people can look at me and instantly tell that I am a little (or maybe a lot) off. Hesitating, I wonder, *do I have on enough makeup to look put together but not so much that I look like I'm trying too hard? Is my hair styled enough to look normal?*

I walk up the sidewalk to the school, desperately trying to get out of my head. I fumble, pulling on door after door until I finally find one that is unlocked. Is everyone watching me? Judging me for clearly not knowing the correct entrance?

Suppressing tears and feelings of inferiority, I walk up to the counter in the school office. "I am here for Ms. Hamilton's class." I sign in and ask for directions. I went to this school as a child but now cannot remember anything about the layout. I follow the lady's verbal instructions to the classroom. As I walk the halls, my mind is racing. *Did I act happy enough when I signed in not to appear depressed? Is anyone actually excited to go to these things? Oh no, was I too happy that it looked like I was faking?*

I'm not sure; however, what I do know is that today, being the best Mom I can be requires showing up for Open House. So, fears and baggage and all, I'm here.

As I walk through the classroom doors, I immediately feel claustrophobic. The room is filled with parents chatting amongst

113

themselves. A few are drilling the teacher with questions. Oh gosh, I don't even have a question. I don't know what goes on at school, except Jordan says he likes it. By the time I've gotten him ready and dropped him off at school, I'm exhausted. I go back home and (thanks to the medications) sleep for a few more hours. I set my alarm to get up in time to go back and get him. I sure don't know what they are learning or who the other kids in the class are. Asking questions and mingling with parents is a little much for me right now. I decide to keep to myself, quiet in the back of the room.

Another parent walks up, sabotaging my attempt to be incognito, and cheerfully declares, "Oh, Hi! You must be Melvin's Mom." I freeze. *Who is Melvin?*

Confused, I slowly reply, "Um, I'm Jordan's Mom." This may not sound like a life-altering conversation, but to someone with severe memory loss, it is terrifying. I've forgotten some pretty big things. I don't trust my perception anymore; maybe I don't even know my child's name.

In a panic, I look down at the desks. Sure enough, on a nametag with pictures of school supplies, red apples, and horizontal dotted lines for learning handwriting, I see printed "Melvin Nash." My heart is racing even faster. I turn to the board. Another list of students in the classroom. Again, "Melvin Nash."

I don't know what to say or do at this point. It is four weeks into the school year. How does everyone know my child's name except me? Finally, I work up the courage to ask the teacher, "Um, just wondering, why does everything say Melvin?"

She casually smiles and replies, "Oh, on the first day of school, he told us, "My name is Jordan, but I go by Melvin.""

I muster up a little, fake chuckle and explain, "Um, he does not actually ever go by Melvin. okay. Thanks. I'll talk to him about it when I get home."

I barely make it back to the sanctuary of my car before bursting into tears. I can't help but realize how far I am behind the other parents. I grieve for what I've lost. I feel terrible that I can't give my kids more. I want to fit in.

I am relieved that I didn't forget Jordan's name. It was my little rascal's stunt, not my memory loss! The tears slowly morph into laughter that Jordan pulled this off; he had an entire class, the teacher, kids, and their parents, calling him Melvin.

As I arrive home and walk through the door, I loudly ask, "Jordan, why is everyone calling you Melvin, and why didn't you tell me?" He explains that there is a skateboarder named Melvin the Nerd, and he thought it would be cool to go by that name. He knew I wouldn't go for it, so the first day of third grade during classroom introductions was the perfect time to implement the name change.

On a deeper level, I realize I need to cut myself a little slack. Today, I wasn't losing it because of my bipolar; I was losing it because of a third-grade boy's not-so-stellar plan. Mental illness or not, life is full of bewildering circumstances, moments of surprise, and slight insanity.

Unfamiliar Faces
October 2011

Since ECT, I have struggled to recognize faces beyond those I see frequently. I run into people who greet me by name. At times, their faces look slightly familiar, and I get the hunch that I know them from somewhere. Other times, I have no frame of reference and no idea if we've ever met.

At church, a middle-aged man approaches, smiling and calling out, "Leah!" I maintain my stiff posture and extend my right arm for a professional handshake. He looks puzzled and utters, "I know you better than that. Come give me a hug." My mouth quivers as I try to fake a smile while leaning in and awkwardly hugging this vaguely familiar face.

This recurring situation is embarrassing and leads to an almost paranoid state. Is there anyone in this room I should know and ought to be acknowledging?

A similar thing happens at Chuck E' Cheese. While chasing Micah, I hear a voice calling my name. I turn around to see a female's face that I know I've seen before, but I haven't the slightest clue where. Again, I don't know how well I know her or what type of relationship we had, and I definitely don't recall her name.

Cheerfully, she asks, "What have you been up to?" Oh no, this is horrible. I don't know who she is or how far to go back.

What have I been up to since when?
I stumble over my words and hurriedly reply, "I went to nursing school and got a job. I got married and had a kid. Then, I transferred to another hospital."

She stops the string of rapid speech, saying, "I know you from the hospital. I work in the lab."

I feel so embarrassed; I went back, like six years too far. The best I can do is hope she doesn't put too much thought into it and laughs off my response as simply not recognizing someone out of context.

Honestly, it's not only her. It is anyone outside of my inner circle. I've forgotten just about everyone. I exit Chuck E' Cheese embarrassed and frustrated.

I Still Struggle to Make Sense of Everything
Journal: January 2012

"What do I believe?
Am I capable of making good logical decisions?
If I just tried harder, would it all be okay?
Am I enough for my children?
Am I capable of being wise with money?
Am I stable?
Is this all really happening?
Am I cursed?
Do I have a purpose that I am able to fulfill?
Can I actually make a difference?
Am I fast enough? Smart enough? Thorough
        enough?
Can I remember enough?
Am I exaggerating, overreacting?
Do I handle stress & situations well?
Could I have prevented all this?
WHY me? WHY us?
When is enough?"

Pecking Fingers, Pecking Order
January 2012

There is a strikingly awkward feeling as I sit down at the computer. I abruptly realize I no longer know my way around the computer programs I previously used on a daily basis. Between the delays of my mental processing, word-finding difficulty, and labored typing, this takes much longer than one might expect. And certainly longer than I'd hoped.

The skill of drafting an email, like many other skills, has faded into the abyss of long-lost memories. I look for clues. The email addressed to me has my name followed by a comma. I copy this format for the reply. Unsure of how many lines to leave, I search the Internet. "How many lines after Dear in an email?" After checking a couple of sources, it seems acceptable to leave a blank line before typing the rest of the email.

The fluid, seventy-word-per-minute typing of my past is gone. I scour the keyboard to locate each letter.

I know there are words for what I want to say; however, I cannot pull forth what they are. I worry that each elementary sentence I type will expose my deficits. I conduct countless Internet searches on formatting, grammar, and spelling before finishing the brief email. I know writing an email never used to be this tedious.

During this phase, I'm continually reverting to an old, deeply ingrained thought: *My worth is based upon what I can do. Now I can't "do."* What little I can do is slow and imperfect.

When all that self-criticism and doubt is stripped away, it leaves a pressing question, *What am I worth now?*

The answer (which is true not only for me but for everyone) is that one's worth is, and will always, be exactly the same. "You are ENOUGH!!" I wish someone would have written, sang, and screamed (possibly even tattooed) this truth.

I don't know what it would have taken for this message to sink in. Maybe my heart was bitter, and my mind was too broken to believe it. But it was, is, and always will be true.

The Handiwork of God
February 2012

Aside from day-to-day skills, many of my talents have faded due to cognitive deficits. Thankfully, my talent for painting remains. After the kids are in bed, I paint canvases to decorate their bedroom. The handmade touch softens the bleak, white apartment walls. The colorful images convey a light-hearted childhood. I know their favorite colors (Micah loves orange, and Jordan favors red) and incorporate their preferences into the paintings.

Maybe it's the artwork and the warm decorations or having my children nearby, but I generally feel safe when we are in each others' presence, inside the walls of our tiny apartment. Our home, sweet home.

But Mother's intuition tells me that something is off lately, particularly with Micah. I know the divorce has been hard on him. The more I ponder, the more neurotic and fearful I become.

My Type A, rational mind is out of answers. There's nothing I can do to patch it, fix it, solve it. I'm left with only one option - prayer. I break down, begging for protection for Micah.

As I walk to the car, I happen to look up at the evening sky. I instantly freeze. The entire sky, every single bit of it, is orange. No red, yellow, pink, or purple, only pure orange.

I feel the message burn within me. "The maker of the sky knows Micah's favorite color. You can paint him pictures, but can you paint the sky his favorite color?"

A sense of peace touches my anxious body. An inner dialogue continues to whisper, "You can paint them pictures, but can you paint the sky his favorite color?"

There is comfort in knowing Micah is noticed. If something as simple as his favorite color is known, certainly his needs are known as well. What is out of my hands is in the mighty hands of the one who controls the sky.

I hold on to this day, this feeling, this message, and it allows me to parent with confidence and worry far less despite my many, many self-perceived shortcomings.

"Don't Duck Mental Health."
March 2012

After school, Jordan begins the ritualistic afternoon backpack purge, pulling out graded papers, broken pencils, hand-drawn comics (that aren't funny because they have boy humor with images of poop and captions like "girls drool"), and remnants of food from snack time.

Today, Jordan pulls out something else. He hands me a paper bag saying, "I made this for you."

I give a customary, "Oh thank you. It's great."

120

As I look closer, it becomes evident this is something different. It's a duck made from a paper bag with a life preserver and a Band-Aid. I flip the duck over to see a small sheet of paper that Jordan has glued onto it. The preprinted title reads "I.C. Hope – Don't Duck Mental Health."

I'm taken aback as I realize they talked about mental illness at his elementary school today. I continue reading the sheet of paper. "The bandage symbolizes that mental illness is real and treatable." "The life preserver represents, 'every life is worth saving'."

This little duck made from a brown paper bag is encouragement from him. In his third-grade mind, I have bipolar that sometimes makes me too happy or too sad and causes me to go to the hospital. He doesn't know the details, but he knows I am sick. Jordan is rooting for me. If I can't do it for myself, I must do it for my kids. I place the paper bag duck on my dresser as a daily reminder that there is hope.

Am I Worthy of the Diagnosis?
March 2012

With increasing flashbacks and nightmares, the doctors agree I need more specific treatment for post-traumatic stress disorder. The anxiety is almost unbearable. My memory is limited still, the emotionally charged memories replay. I have frequent flashbacks of being helpless and abused, both as a teenager and in my failed marriage.

121

I jump at the tiniest scare. One night, Jordan thought it would be funny to hide around the corner of our short apartment hallway. He was supposed to be in bed but had snuck out for one last joke. Jordan is always up for a little scandal.

As I'm winding down for the night with the TV remote in my hand, ready to watch an episode of something/anything to slow my mind before sleep, I hear a loud "Boo!" Before my mind can even process, I've jumped while simultaneously whacking my child across the head with the remote as hard as I can.

My hyperarousal, due to PTSD, abruptly thwarts Jordan's prank. Zero to one hundred real quick. Of course, I feel terrible. Jordan precedes to tell his friends of the story when his Mom hit him in the head with a remote, stating, "Mom has really bad reflexes, but she can't help it." He and his friends laugh. I do not.

Regardless of my emotional pain and the severe impact on daily life, I struggle to accept the diagnosis.

> Journal: I feel guilty to claim I have PTSD. I don't feel my trauma has been severe enough to be in the same category as soldiers & POWs. I think I should just get over it. If I can't get over it, then it should be called something else.

The nightmares continue. I am afraid to sleep. When I finally get to sleep, I wake in a sweat-covered panic. I live in a state of fear and impending doom.

Venting
June 2012

Journal: "I am pleased to remember my SSN. Proud to know my children's birthdays. Excited to know my way around the roads of my hometown. I can even figure out how to fill out a blank check. Definite progress.

Unfortunately, all this amazing progress has been made in about the last year. I still lack the vivid memory that I used to have. At least I can retain a good percentage of what I have seen and done in the past year. I can't for the life of me remember who I have told what. I try to get around it by silence or just asking, "I told you about ___, right?"

The part that frightens me the most is that the other years of my life are gone. Except for scary or sad times. Totally gone. Oh, how I wish I had them back! I don't remember the first house I bought, my kids' births or birthdays, graduations, vacations, jokes, holidays, helping others, school & subjects. I even have a hard time remembering how to spell. Movies, people's names, surgeries, jobs... gone. I feel like I stared at the "Men in Black" forget light too long... way too long.

What will help? How to help? WHY? Where do I go from here? Stepping-stones vs. washed out to sea? Who the hell knows?"

{two steps forward,
one devastating step back}

Uncle Gary, Too
June 2012

There is something about feeling understood by another individual walking a similar path. Although you'd never wish this type of pain and suffering on someone else, it's nice not to have to explain. They just get it on a deeply personal level, without you having to say a word.

Uncle Gary's move from out West to the deep South was not always the fairytale chapter of life he had dreamed of. However, I greatly appreciate his companionship. Through long talks on the front porch, Uncle Gary and I got closer than I ever thought would be possible with a relative. He was the missing piece, the family connection I had always wanted growing up.

Uncle Gary is the one who could handle anything. He was the one I called when I accidentally put Diesel instead of unleaded in my car. With his incredible skills, he fixed everything I broke. On the one hand, he held my secrets, and on the other hand, he knew how to make me laugh.

It is 11:30 a.m. I have dropped Jordan off at football camp and am back at the apartment when the phone rings. It's Dad. As I answer, he checks to see how I am feeling. I recognize it. Dad is fishing to see if I am stable enough to take some bad news? I assure him I am.

Dad says, "Uncle Gary killed himself today."

My heart stops, and my feet give out from under me as my body drops to the ground. Curled in the fetal position, all I can do is wail, "No, no, no."

After a few minutes, I finally ask, "What happened?" Dad informs me that Uncle Gary's neighbor called the police after he heard a gunshot in the woods, which backup to their condos.

Uncle Gary shot himself.

In disbelief, I blurt out, "I don't understand. We talked on the phone for over an hour just a few days ago. He said he was doing so much better. The meds and the therapy were working."

Over the next few hours, my emotions quickly alternate between intense sorrow and rage. Uncle Gary was my partner on this treacherous journey. We had an agreement that we were going to do whatever it took to get treatment, and he lied to me. Even that last stupid phone call was, in actuality, his goodbye.

He misled me, saying he was better.

He quit on me!

I cry and cry until it's time to pick Jordan up from football. I cry as I drive. I cry as I park. I pull it together long enough to say my child's name to the camp leader organizing pickup. As I wait for Jordan to come out, an old acquaintance walks up and jokingly nudges my arm. "Smile. You look so sad."

My mind races. *Do you know I just got the worst news in a long time, maybe my life? My favorite relative, the only one who gets what I'm going through, my partner in this madness shot himself in the head today. I don't know how to function or how to continue. I don't know if I can even keep going without him. And I am supposed to smile right now?*

But I can't say that. Of all the good things bipolar has taught me, it has also taught me some not-so-good things. I have learned how to be theatrically fake in the midst of terrible pain. So, I keep silent and flash the most unnatural, forced smile and a little "hehe" giggle.

Jordan walks down the sidewalk and out of football camp. We make it to the car. I manage to close the car door before bursting into tears again. I have to tell him Uncle Gary is dead.

Trials (Of Life and the Legal System)
June 2012

My divorce attorney, Kevin, looks at me as I walk through the metal detector at the entrance of the courthouse, blatantly inquiring, "What are you on?"

I am taken aback. I realize I must look almost as bad as I feel. "Nothing. I'm not on anything." I clarify, "I'm so nervous I haven't slept."

This day in court is the day I have been dreading. The day I'm not sure if I will make it through. Samuel, my ex, has intentionally postponed this day for three years, making every step of the divorce as time-consuming and expensive as possible. With zero insight into his contributions, he insists that the judge deny the divorce in hopes that I will change my mind.

But, I also realize if I do survive this day, this could be one of those days that has the power to change an entire life, maybe even generations. Today is the day I will testify and fight for my freedom. I must speak my truth, so my children and I will have the best chance at an emotionally healthy future.

Due to the sensitive nature of the hearing, it has been determined that it will be a closed courtroom. Witnesses will wait outside.

I sit next to my attorney. His masculine demeanor and tall stature feel protective.

My eyes skim a large but relatively empty courtroom. Inevitably, I see Samuel. I wonder what is crossing his mind. All I can think is, I just want out.

After a few opening remarks, I am ushered to the seat next to the judge. It's time for my testimony. I raise my trembling hand while repeating the verbiage to be sworn in. Everything in me is exhausted and wants to quit.

His attorney starts. I answer question after question. Hundreds of pages of highly sensitive medical records have been subpoenaed. I try to give enough information to satisfy, but I know there are holes in my story. There are holes in every bit of my life.

Samuel's attorney attempts to disqualify my testimony, questioning how the memories of what Samuel put me through could be vivid, but I have forgotten other memories. I try to explain it is a different type of memory, a frightening one filled with emotional pain, and although these memories are ones I wish I could forget, I can't.

I'm filled with worry. I know what Samuel's attorney is doing; trying to prove my testimony is nothing more than a fabrication by an unstable woman and unfit mother.

After an hour of intense questioning, I return to my seat. Samuel now gives his testimony. He sits tall, gleaming in his chair, as if this day, his moment in the spotlight, is what he had been waiting for. As if this would be the day that would clear up all misunderstandings, and I would somehow return. Samuel proudly refutes my claims. "I was never controlling. I let her eat at two restaurants." He continues to arrogantly tell of all of his imposed restrictions, from not allowing friends in the house, to obsessively looking for crumbs, to demanding I not drink a soft drink, all the while maintaining that these regulations were in my best interest. Samuel begs the judge to deny me the right to attend my own church.

I wonder what the judge hears as he listens to Samuel ramble, seemingly digging his own grave. But then again, I wonder how one weighs his claims versus my medical records. The attorneys call additional witnesses and place pictures and journals into evidence. The attorneys go back and forth.

I'm thankful my attorney can fight on my behalf. I don't have any fight left in me.

After a full day, court is adjourned. It will be weeks before the judge will render the verdict. I am left with no choice but to wait and see. Will my mental illness disqualify me from being perceived as a fit parent? Do numerous hospitalizations mean I shouldn't be allowed to care for my child?

With my stomach in knots and physically exhausted, I walk to the car knowing I've given all I can for today and that will have to do for now.

Legacy
July 2012

My thoughts are overwhelmed with the complex legal system and pending divorce. The fear leaves my stomach nauseated and anxiety sky high. Even so, these feelings are more pleasant than where my mind goes when left alone to wander.

Uncle Greg's face — a visibly warped reminder of a gunshot wound at rock bottom.

The loss of Aunt Gabrielle.

And now, Uncle Gary is gone as well.

Unable to properly cope, compartmentalizing is the only way to attempt to overshadow deep pain. It doesn't matter. The messages are subconsciously ingrained.

We, the Nashs as a species, are not made for survival.

When life gets tough, suicide is a viable and often-utilized option.

You are not better than the relatives who have gone before you and therefore, you are vulnerable. Suicide may likely be your future.

I can fight mental illness with everything within me; however, these nagging thoughts remain, lying and waiting within the fibers of my being.

Say Hello Like a Politician
July 2012

I continue to feel the impact of ECT on nearly all aspects of my functioning, including my social life. I strive to make people feel important and appreciated, but I don't remember them. I can't count the number of times I've introduced myself saying, "Nice to meet you" to people I have known for years.

It is embarrassing for me, and I worry about how they feel. I want to protect them from the rejection of being forgotten. Later on, I find an excellent strategy for handling this.

While watching television, I notice a politician greet someone, saying, "Nice to see you." That's it! This will be my new, socially acceptable replacement for "Nice to meet you." That phrase gets me in far too much trouble when I use it on people I should know but don't recognize. I strategize... say hello like a politician. From now on, I vow never to say, "Nice to meet you again." It will always be, "Nice to see you."

Knuckle-deep
July 2012

After months of chatting on skate park bleachers, Tommy continues to provide company throughout difficult times.

Hoping to spend some time together off duty, Tommy invites me to join him for frozen yogurt. Even the invite alone is surprising. I keep thinking, this will be the moment he nicely tells me I am too much to handle.

As we sit down in the bistro chairs with our mounds of frozen yogurt and every candy known to man, we chat as comfortably as long-time friends. We've talked about so many heavy topics on the sidelines of the skate park that we can get to the light stuff now. We swap funny stories from high school (mine are limited, so I mostly listen to his), talk about our hopes for the future, and goofily quote lyrics from old rap songs.

As we are chatting, he laughs, "You have ice cream on your hand."

Sure enough, my knuckles are covered in chocolate. I dug into the bowl a little too enthusiastically. I'm embarrassed but quickly remind myself... *This is you: flaws and all. A lot of this is up to him.*

It's not a fear of being unladylike or lacking a few manners. It is much deeper than that. It is a fear of who I've become overall - the insecure, unstable young woman before him. I can't help but fear he will run at any time.

Purpose in Pain?

August 2012

It's been a few years since my lowest point. I am surprised that I am even considering there may have been a tiny bit of good or purpose in all the pain. What has shifted that I would even consider this? I've always thought of bipolar and the associated struggles as my burden to endure.

Now I am exploring the idea that I, or someone around me, may benefit from what I have been through. I sincerely hope it is true. I don't want all the suffering to have been in vain. Now, I still don't know what the possible good could be, but I vow to be open and aware of how this disorder and the memory loss could have changed me for the better.

Engaged: In My Own Life
August 2012

I was sure the last hospital admission was "goodbye for just a bit ." Frequent admissions seemed to have been my pattern; however, over the past year, I have been learning some new skills: Recognizing feelings, practicing mindfulness, and accepting the seemingly unacceptable.

Days, weeks, and months have passed without feeling suicidal. It isn't like a switch happened to flip one day. It has been a much more subtle process. It is becoming evident the last hospitalization may have been the last. If not the last forever, at least the last for a while.

It is certainly not a sign of weakness or failure to seek help. It is, however, a pleasant surprise to endure the storms of life while remaining relatively stable and positively engaged in my own life.

Paradigm Shift in Prayer
October 2012

Despite a gradual upswing, my faith continues to waver. When I can't make sense of it all, I question God. When I have no one left to blame, I blame God. When I'm frustrated beyond reason, I curse God.

Being bitter and unsuccessful in the spiritual realm is utterly exhausting. Although I've tried to go at it alone, I've found the burden is too heavy to bear. I long for a change of heart. I genuinely don't want to spend my life mad at God, but at this point, I don't know if I can trust Him.

Journal: "I realize that I am kinda moving from a place where my prayers probably need an edited, bleeped out version to a searching, a wounded, manipulated, scared & filtered hunger... Change is in the air at a much-needed time. I am worn out on a soul level. Yah, there are a lot of great times, but deep down I am exhausted with heavy burden. What better time than now to ask for some help, wisdom, guidance?"

Short-Lived Victory
October 2012

My attorney calls. The judge has made his ruling; he has ruled in my favor. I am granted the title of the primary custodial parent. Samuel will see Micah three days a week, but I didn't lose my rights.

It feels like a huge victory; however, the feeling of impending doom quickly overshadows the success. If I know Samuel, he will not quit that easily.

Sure enough, within a matter of weeks, I get word from my attorney that Samuel has taken the divorce to the state appellate court. *Are you freaking kidding me?* Now, it will take even longer before Samuel's petition to stay married, and in control, will ultimately be denied. I just want this to end.

Can Education Save?
November 2012

It has become increasingly clear that Plan A (nursing) is not and can never be an option for me again. I simply don't remember enough to do my job. I cry as I defeatedly throw away the renewal form, officially allowing my license to expire.

It is also devastating to think of life on disability.

I've always thought of education as a ticket out of dire situations. I got an associate's degree when faced with being a teen parent. Now faced with a lifetime of disability, I fall back on education as well.

I spend days doing online career tests - the free versions, of course, because who has money to pay for career testing when they have no job? Finally, I end up with an intricate web of printed test results. Printouts detailing my various strengths, weaknesses, and values span the bedroom floor.

I see a page with a "you might like these jobs" section. An alternate career in the healthcare realm is among the many choices. I know little about the profession, but I remember working with some individuals in this field in the hospital.

That might be cool. I could still be in the medical field without needing all the nursing knowledge I've lost.

Over the next few days, I will do more research. I am terrified and uncertain if my "new" just-discovered Plan B will even work - the desire to avenge all that's been lost wells up inside of me. I'm going for it.

Based on my transcript from ten years ago, as the uninjured, mentally stable Honor Roll Leah, I am quickly accepted into a program that will start in the spring. First, I will need a bachelor's and ultimately a master's degree.

Counting My Blessings in the Form of Free Food
November 2012

It is Wednesday, the day before Thanksgiving. The holiday hustle and bustle is in full swing. Displays of frequently used ingredients for a delicious Thanksgiving dinner fill the grocery store, but I can't afford any of it. There simply isn't money for anything extra this year.

As I'm going about my usual morning routine of chasing children and trying to pick up the house, I hear a knock on the apartment door. I turn the knob to find a smiling family of five. The kids are holding numerous reusable shopping bags filled with groceries. The father and mother are holding Cracker Barrel boxes filled with everything needed for a large family meal - turkey, green beans, mashed potatoes, rolls, and an entire pie! You name it. I discover that a nonprofit organization that provided us with canned goods and covered an electric bill a few months ago has included us in their Thanksgiving meal drive.

I repeatedly thank the family who took the time and courage to make it to our apartment, through the community, decorated with gang graffiti and open drug and alcohol use on the sidewalk, to bring us an incredible meal.

As I often do when touched by unforeseen blessings, I cry. I am beyond thankful, as there was no budget for an extravagant Thanksgiving meal for my family.

At the same time, there is a strange sense of disappointment. How have I gotten to this place? I used to be the one donating to charities and volunteering at events. Now, after giving it my all, I can't even help myself, let alone others.

We are barely making it.

I Didn't Know I Needed to Feel Small
January 2013

This moment is unbelievable - sitting on a cruise ship in the middle of the Caribbean. I pinch myself, and it's real. It's been years since my last vacation, as I didn't dare consider spending bill money on anything frivolous. Obviously, the Caribbean was out of the question.

Yet, here I am. Victoria, one of those who have stuck with me through the roughest times, didn't give me a choice. She informed me that I was going on the cruise because she'd already paid my way - airfare, cruise costs, everything.

It's late now, and the crowds have meandered back to their rooms. I hear nothing but the crashing of the waves and the humming of the cruise ship engines. An uncanny peacefulness has replaced the worries of daily life.

The boat that looked enormous in the port now feels minuscule out at sea. I look into the darkness from the top deck, nothing but water in all directions. My mind continues to wander as

I imagine all the creatures swimming below. I wonder how deep the ocean is at this point. I think of the people living on distant islands. The daydreams this evening are endless.

I feel so small. Tears slowly roll down my cheeks. I didn't know it, but I've desperately needed to feel small. Back home, my troubles seem overwhelmingly large, but here, I feel like a tiny part of the vastness of the world. There is no way for the magnitude of my troubles to even compete with the seemingly endless horizon. I've been engulfed in my own story.

But, at this moment, I feel renewed. It is comforting to know the world is bigger than my problems. Then again, it is the dichotomy that I and my troubles are small; however, the Creator of this vast ocean sees tiny me, that He would be mindful of this little speck on the pool deck of a ship in the middle of the Caribbean.

This is hopeful; this trip - this moment - is what I needed.

Rusty to Rapid
January 2013

It has been many years since my last college course. I go through the distantly familiar routines of getting textbooks and reading syllabi. My first few semesters will be online, something I've never done before. A decade ago, there was no such thing. There's a bit of a culture shock - posting on discussion boards and properly citing resources; However, it doesn't take long to become familiarized with this system. I appreciate that coursework can be done from the kitchen table, saving drive time and avoiding that inevitable classmate who wants to ask an ungodly amount of questions. I can go at my own pace, lightning speed.

More of Tommy
February 2013

I'm sure one could argue that I am in no condition to be dating. The dynamics might reveal old patterns and my need to focus on myself first. The truth is, it feels incredible to have someone want me. Of course, I have precious friends who treasure me, but it's different.

I have always believed that I'm too much to handle. Being single reinforces this. However, having someone romantically interested in me refutes this belief and sprinkles hope throughout my day. I optimistically daydream about Tommy. Each text brings a bit of hope that I might not have to walk this debilitating journey alone.

Tommy has become my someone.

Tommy and I are beginning to spend more time together. His work hours have dwindled - not the best financially, but perfect for a new couple in love. We have plenty of time to enjoy each other's company. We go to the county fair, see movies at noon, eat sushi, paint pictures, hike trails, and "snuggle."

This relationship is different from anything I've ever experienced. There is love without control, excitement without smothering, and appreciation without conformity. I'm giddy.

D-I-S-A-B-L-E-D
March 2013

I receive an official-looking letter from the Social Security
Administration. I anxiously open the envelope. I've been approved
for disability benefits based on the pay rate of my previous nursing
job, for $1 shy of the maximum allowable amount.

I should be excited and relieved. Instead, my stomach turns,
and my heart sinks as I stare at the letter.

The government of the United States of America thinks I
am disabled.

There were no additional questions. No convincing. No
appeal is necessary. Maybe I didn't do as well as I thought on all the
psychiatrist's questions. Perhaps I am worse off than I know. I cry. I
dishearteningly face reality - I am useless and everyone, including the
government, knows it.

At twenty-six years old, I sign up for Medicare and my
AARP prescription rider. I am officially lumped into the "disabled
and elderly" demographic.

Not Enough Time to Lie
April 2013

While out and about, I notice a familiar face. I am surprised I
recognize this lady, as this is more than I can usually recall. She is the
supervisor from an old job. My ex-husband still works there, and I
can only imagine the rumors he spreads to avoid personal fault. His
typical story involves telling all who will listen that his wife became
mentally ill and left him.

The supervisor also recognizes me, asking, "How have you been?"

Internally, I freeze. She has likely heard the rumors circulating of my mental illness. I can't lie and say I am still nursing. I share the truth for some reason, or maybe just the lack of time to think of a good lie. "I've been alright. I got diagnosed with bipolar, and it has been really hard."

She doesn't even miss a beat and encouragingly says, "Bipolar isn't too bad once you find the right medication combination." That's it. She changes topics, and we laugh about the kids' latest mischief.

Internally, I'm still stuck on "not too bad." *What? How is bipolar not too bad? It has been absolute hell!*

Everything in me longs to believe her. I guess it's true; with each medication dud, we have gotten a step closer to finding what might work. I replay her statement over and over in my mind, longing for it to be true, "Bipolar isn't too bad once you find the right medication combination."

The Goal is Not to Get Back What Was Lost
June 2013

I spend most of my emotional energy focusing on regaining what was lost. Then I realize there is a flaw in this thought process. The goal should not be to get back what was lost. The focus should be on forward progress. This idea seems simple, and yet, it is a game-changer, a revelation.

Because of the memory loss, my mind continually attempts to fill in the gaps. I remember the historic house I bought after filing for divorce with great fondness - the white picket fence and the skeleton key to the front door.

But, it's strange. I am gathering that this period was not as rosy as my mind painted it.

While looking at a photograph of the historic home, Dad commented, "That was a very dark time. You started having trouble within a month or two of moving into that house."

Dad's summary was shocking news; however, it makes sense the more I think about it. I wasn't even in the house a year before suicide attempts, multiple hospitalizations, and the loss of my job (the only means of making a house payment).

Realizing the peak of my existence, being the proud homeowner of the most charming home, was the moment I was struggling to regain.

Being submerged in shock and sorrow leads to a moment of epiphany. The goal is not to get back what was lost. I repeat this to myself because it's evident that the past was darker than I remember. Seeking to regain the foreclosed house, the lost job, and the mental acuity that I used to have keeps me trapped in a victim mentality.

The goal is to move forward with the expectation of new gifts, perhaps greater gifts. Forward-thinking brings new freedom as I accept that the future will never look the same as the past. There will, however, be new dreams and new laughter and new gratitude.

Screw Happy Quotes
August 2013

I have come to accept that I don't do well with "happy" quotes. I'm not sure when it became socially acceptable to post nauseating, idealistic sayings all over the place.

I drive in my car, and I see bumper stickers. "It's gonna be all right." I ask a friend if it's a crime to spray paint "WHEN? When is it going to be all right?" on someone's car. She chuckles, but I'm serious.

I walk around town and read other people's shirts proudly displaying vomitous optimism. "Life is Good." How is this possible? YOUR life may be good, but there is no way in the world I am wearing that shirt. My shirt would read, "Life is hard as hell!!" What are the purposes of these sayings anyway? They are not convincing me of anything except my life must be even worse than I initially thought. Certainly worse than the person wearing the shirt or driving the car with the bumper sticker. The feelings of isolation increase. Again.

While browsing in a craft store, I stop to look at wall decals. One of them reads, "Live well. Laugh much. Love often." Vomit. Why can't I get away from these sayings and the constant reminders that I must be doing something gravely wrong?

I struggle to make it through a full day at this point, let alone do it well. I cry much. That isn't on the decal. And I do love often - to the best of my ability - which currently means being irritable, not calling people back, and forgetting all meaningful things happening in my loved ones' lives.

While reading, I run across, "Life is hard - not because we're doing it wrong, just because it's hard." - Glennon Doyle. Thank you! It's not another saying that life is marvelous and continually full of bliss. Someone finally gets it. The authenticity of this resonates with my soul.

Maybe I am not the only one struggling after all. From that point forward, I hold on to meaningful, genuine quotes. The quotes begin to form a sense of community, a shared vulnerability that increases my feeling of connectedness.

Armchair Psychologist
July 2014

I'm developing a love for psychology. I take an extra psychology class every time I get the chance, although I don't plan to use any of it formally. I'm looking for anything that can help me improve my life skills - taking the new information and applying it to myself.

I watch and listen with the utmost attention hoping to absorb wisdom sprinkled throughout the lecture. For example, a professor who is a psychologist shared that when depressed, it is helpful to go outside. Tall, mature trees draw the eye upward, and it is difficult to be as depressed when looking upward. Who knew?

Today, the same instructor tells of a client who chose a different path than she personally would have taken. The professor warns of giving advice or judging others based upon what we would do. She shares the most simple sentence with the most profound impact: "If you had the same genetics and were raised in the same environment and had the same experiences, you would do the exact same thing every time."

I fight back the tears. The class continues around me as if nothing happened - as if the entire universe hadn't just shifted beneath our desks. I don't know if the other students are even paying attention, but this moment is earth-shattering for me. Her words replay in my mind. I REALLY need to internalize this. I would never deny that others are fighting a hard battle or criticize how they handle it; however, I'd never allow myself that grace. I negate the difficulty of my journey and shower myself in "shoulds"... like internally "shoulding" all over myself.

Leah, you should remember more. You should have more money by now. You should have known better. You should be able to get over this.

But with the professor's mindset, "shoulds" take on a different meaning. Even my worst choices and enormous failures SHOULD have happened. They are not an exclusive personal failure; they would have happened to anyone with my genetics, environment, and experiences.

The simple sentence is life-altering, not only for my recovery but also in terms of my capacity for self-forgiveness.

Creative Juices Flowing
March 2014

For me, manic episodes don't occur nearly as often as depressive episodes. Depressive episodes are relatively frequent, getting me in trouble as my self-worth crumbles and the internal loud-speaker of hopelessness overpowers my mind. *Give up. The world is better off without you. Things will never change.*

Mania appears in a different, typically unrecognizable fashion. Some episodes come on rapidly, while others are more gradual. The depression lifts.

Oh God, it feels good to have those thoughts (that are almost mentally loud enough to be voices) silenced. Manic episodes surface under the guise of hope. *You got this. I don't know why you ever doubted yourself. The world is full of possibilities; seize the moment. Go for it. You can't fail.* At this stage, I don't see it. I just feel good.

For many years, I valued manic episodes as a welcome compensation for the horrific depths of depression. (I would have never believed that someday, way down the line, mania would land me in the hospital.) Now, I feel the universe owes me energy to compensate for and complete the unfinished tasks lingering from the previous depressive state.

I place trash bags over the kitchen table, making an improvised drop cloth. I pull out art supplies scattering them across the makeshift, horizontal easel.

So many creative ideas flood in all at once that it's hard to know where to begin. There is no time to sketch an outline; this is flowing from sheer talent. I will paint an ocean scene. I've never worked with oils, only acrylics, but that doesn't worry me. *Why didn't I think of this before?* My artistic skills are exceptional, or so I think.

I have to tell Dad; he works in finance, so he'll be thrilled with this new business idea. I dial the phone as I haphazardly squirt blue and white paint onto my palette (a paper plate).

Dad answers on the other end. Before he can finish the word "Hello," I blurt out with rapid speech, "I just figured out how I'm going to make money. I'm going to paint pictures and sell them online. I've already created a profile. Oh, and I'm going to give 10% to charity. This generosity will help everyone. I'm already starting on my first painting. I'm going to paint oceans and trees and birds and flowers. I'm even going to use recycled materials for some of the paintings." Dad doesn't ask many questions. He simply listens.

"Alright Dad, well, I gotta go. I'm painting an ocean right now. Love you. Bye."

I glance at the clock, perfect. It's 10:45 p.m. The kids are sleeping and won't interfere with my master plan of masterpieces.

My mind races faster than my hand can brush. The canvas takes a little while to cover. I've picked a canvas size congruent with my grand plan, 50" x 40." I paint with faster and faster brush strokes, rushing to produce merchandise for my new online store. My midnight art is the solution to all our financial troubles; I just wish I had thought of it sooner.

The ocean waves are apparent. The sky is satisfactory. Now, at 3:50 a.m., the painting requires white clouds and foam on the ocean waves. The urgency is indescribable. There is no time to allow the layers of oil paints to dry. I dab as carefully as possible. The masterpiece is something to behold.

I step back, now noticing the smell of newness and paint fumes. The mental tsunami is starting to slow a little. Only now do I

149

feel the fatigue in my body. It hits me. My whirlwind of an art project needs to come to a halt. There are only a few hours until the kids will wake. I haven't eaten dinner. I forgot to take my evening medications. I pop a few pills with a glass of water while pouring some paint thinner to clean the brushes.

The sun is starting to rise. I still can't sleep, but I notice the medications beginning to work. My mind begins processing at a slightly slower speed.

Oh crap, I've done it again. A sinking feeling ushers me back to reality. The business plan isn't going to save my finances. I'll probably never even follow through with getting a painting up on the website. This ocean picture is acceptable for a first experiment with oils, but it certainly isn't gallery-worthy. (It will later sell for $5 at a garage sale.)

Now it makes sense why Dad didn't say more on the phone. Another manic plan that sounded foolproof to me, but he saw right through it. The lingering effects of mania cushion the blow of reality.

The soft voice of reason whispers, *There's nothing you can do about the failed business plan right now. Let the painting dry and try to get some rest before the kids wake.*

Run With Endurance
April 2014

Depression tells me I shouldn't get out of bed. The psychiatric medications have side effects of lethargy and weight gain. My lithium-induced hypothyroidism says I will be slow and overweight.

I've had enough and am fighting back - like the kid who has been bullied too long. I can't even run 100 meters, but I've decided fighting back looks like running a half marathon. I get fitted for running shoes with custom insoles, workout pants, and headphones. As I scroll through the Internet searching terms such as "Can't run to running a half-marathon," I find a running schedule that details how much to run and on which days.

I start by running from one mailbox to the next, walking after each short interval. I run for a song and walk for a song to switch things up. I can't even fathom how far 13.1 miles is right now.

But I feel the urge to combat - stop being a victim of mental illness, and take charge. I, for whatever reason, am still here today. When I am running with all I have - the blood pounding, gasping for air, sore legs   I feel more alive than ever. Slowly, the workouts get longer, and I get stronger.

Medication Compliant
July 2014

I finally feel well. Not too manically great and not too depressingly bad. Right smack dab in the middle of normal. My first thought is: the meds must be working.

I flashback to nursing school. Memories are scattered, but I remember a few sentences from a lecture in our psychiatric nursing class. "Sometimes psychiatric patients will start to feel better, and they will think they have been healed and stop taking their medications. It was the medication working that made them feel

151

better." I don't remember much more of the lecture except that she mentioned the high rates of noncompliance within this population.

Strange, isn't it. This flashback of a lecture is the ONLY lecture I remember from nursing school. These sentences were ingrained years before I knew I would need this information for myself. These sentences survived the memory loss. Sometimes, I wonder if I went to nursing school for that bit of information. Was that the key to my compliance and my future?

I'm proud to say I've never stopped taking prescriptions on my own. As terrible as the side effects have been, I've refused to stop without calling and speaking to my psychiatrist first. Honestly, I would be horrified if my chart said, "noncompliant."

{loving life - even when it is brutal}

Not Even Out the Gate and Already Struggling Educationally
August 2014

I have completed my bachelor's but have many semesters left ahead, that is assuming I can even get accepted into graduate school. Most of the day, the kids are in school, which leaves me plenty of time to study for the graduate school entrance exam. I've picked up two incredibly thick books to review. I only have to take one or the other - the MAT or the GRE.

I've heard the MAT is not as hard, so I pull that book from my bag. I skip the intro and go directly to chapter one. The first few pages discuss crossing out wrong answers to increase the odds of choosing a correct answer. Makes sense. I'm feeling slightly more confident. Quickly, I'm on to chapter two. My head begins to spin as I realize how lost I am. I have no idea what any of these words mean. To make matters worse, the example questions are incredibly complicated.

Why are all the questions in this stupid format? It hits me. Oh my gosh, Miller ANALOGIES Test. I'm not sure why, but I have extreme difficulty with analogies since ECT. They don't make sense when others use them, and they are out of my vocabulary altogether. I spend the entire day hoping one more page or one more example in this stupid book will help.

Maybe graduate school will never work, and I should quit now. But how can someone base my full capability of making it through school on my worst thing, analogies?

I feel utterly defeated. Nothing helps. I go to bed feeling like my chance of making it to graduate school is dwindling. The recurring fear of being found out, of being discovered as mentally ill and inadequate, surfaces.

One Way or Another - At Least I Will Know I Tried
August 2014

I feel like lying around moping, but the tiny fighter in me refuses to sit back and do nothing. Apprehensively, I pull out the other book for the entrance exam - the GRE. I check what the abbreviation stands for, ensuring it doesn't have to do with analogies. Graduate Record Examinations: that sounds a tad better. I flip through the book. The many topics increase my odds.

I am most worried about the essay portion. I study common topics; however, grammatically and formatting-wise, I've forgotten most of what I learned in English classes. I typically rely on spell check and a thesaurus. Neither will be available during the test. My vocabulary is limited, and words frequently escape me.

My attempt to get into graduate school is probably never going to work. But I have to give it my all, so even if it fails, I know I tried my hardest. At this point, it's all about acknowledging my limitations but living without regret.

Party of Four, Considering Party of Five
September 2014

Tommy and I have grown incredibly close. We don't have anything official like a ring, but the four of us (Tommy, Jordan, Micah, and I) have all started to feel like a family. Tommy continues to step-parent despite the kids' tests of his dedication. I feel blessed to have him by my side.

But where do we go from here? Due to financial aid restrictions, we can't get married while I'm in school. Tommy and I have been co-parenting the two kiddos, but we've started talking about another baby. I can't quite explain it, but our family doesn't feel complete, and the prospect of a new addition to the family sounds like the solution.

Tommy and I decide we will go sans birth control and see what happens.

Dedicating Miles of the Half Marathon
October 2014

It's unseasonably cold at 35 degrees. Dressing for the half marathon, I wrap my face in ski gear, trying to avoid an asthma attack triggered by the cold.

Something else is off. I feel a little sluggish and queasy, like I'm coming down with something. I have to go through with this race. I have trained way too hard, and I need to prove this to myself. I stretch and prepare my playlist.

It's 7 a.m., and we are off. As the endorphins flood my body, I start to get a little emotional. A single tear runs down my cheek. Not a sad tear. A "Hell no, it's about to get real because I'm giving it my all" tear. This race is about so much more than burning calories or sexy legs.

This is personal. This is about my journey. I run a mile for each family member I have lost due to suicide. Emotions are high, but it isn't anger-driven; it is intense hope that circumstances can't squash. I run another mile to show my strength despite what I've been through with my ex-husband. I run a mile for the people who thought I'd quit with teen pregnancy. I run a mile for each of my kids who have witnessed the ups and downs. This is the feeling of resilience - a purpose that previous failures cannot extinguish. I run a mile for my future. Before I know it, I've run all 13.1 miles in a little over two hours.

I learn my body is capable of so much more than I'd ever dreamed. I realize what it feels like to be a fighter. And a darn good one, at that.

{new life, new fears}

High Risk
October 2014

Sure enough, there is a reason for feeling different on the day of the half marathon, and ever since. That extra snuggling has led to a positive pregnancy test. I didn't honestly think I would get pregnant the first month without birth control. A mixture of excitement and concern floods my mind. My first concern is if the baby will even be alright. My medications are considered high risk during pregnancy with documented cases of congenital disabilities. This whole thing, pregnant and bipolar, is new to me. I wasn't diagnosed or on any medications with the older two.

I call the moment Dr. Morris' morning phone lines open. But I don't know how to convey the news. A baby is always good news, right? But is it in this situation, with my condition and medications?

The receptionist takes my information, "Do you mind if I place you on hold while I check with the doctor?" A couple of minutes pass. She returns to the line, "The doctor said to stop all of your medications and make an appointment immediately."

Since my diagnosis, I've never been off medications, not even for a day. *This is already frightening. What have I gotten myself into?*

The following day, I walk into the doctor's office for the first appointment of my pregnancy - not with the obstetrician as had been the case with my other pregnancies pre mental illness, but with the psychiatrist. Dr. Morris carefully calculates the weeks of exposure to lithium. The main concern is for cardiac defects related

161

to exposure during the first few weeks of pregnancy. I will receive additional monitoring by the high-risk obstetrician.

There is another dilemma - what to do for medication. The pharmaceutical candidate must provide an adequate level of mood stabilization and the lowest risk to the baby. Although I had been on multiple medications, a low dose monotherapy will have to suffice.

I can accept the pregnancy may be a little rocky, possibly on too low of a dosage to do the trick for me. I struggle to accept that my illness could negatively impact the baby. People attempt to console me, saying things such as, "You have to put your oxygen mask on first before someone else's." Or "People do much worse while they are pregnant and their kids turn out fine." I don't care to hear these condolences.

I tremble and worry with every appointment.

Wishing Me a Merry Christmas Won't Touch This Level of Misery
December 2014

"It's the most wonderful time of the year."

"Tis the season to be jolly."

"Joy to the world."

This time of year, the messages to be joyful overwhelm. It isn't as simple as singing a Christmas carol to brighten the mood. As I douse the yard in Christmas lights, I also pull out the lightbox. The dermatologist likes it better than my old bootleg version, the tanning bed.

Even with lightbox sessions at lunchtime and a heaping handful of vitamin D supplements daily, it will likely be a few months before I feel anything close to joy. The gray winter skies have merged with my innermost being. Numb and heavy feelings have taken over my body, causing me to go about my day in a slow, robotic fashion.

Long after the holiday season has ended, the warmth of the sunshine will eventually permeate this empty feeling. Seasons will change, and as I've learned, moods will change as well.

It May Not Be a Bank Holiday, But It's Legit
February 2015

Pregnant and struggling, I'm in desperate need of a new way to barely function. I summon the kids into the living room. "Guys, so today is National Lazy Day."

With confused faces, they inquire, "What's that?"

I confidently declare, "National Lazy Day is a day where no one is allowed to do anything. No cleaning, no laundry, and no driving anywhere except to get ice cream. Ice cream and TV are the ONLY things you're allowed to do. Reheating leftovers is pushing it, but there definitely isn't any cooking."

The kids seem pleasantly surprised. The children don't ask who declared National Lazy Day (which would have been an easy answer - a pregnant woman who doesn't have the energy to brush her hair) or how often this occurs (which again would have been an easy question to address - whenever I need it to).

So, without any questions, we go straight to observing National Lazy Day. We lie on the sofa watching old movies for hours. Nobody lifts a finger until it's time for a heaping scoop of ice cream.

Happy National Lazy Day! And cheers to doing whatever it takes to get through the day.

Tiny Heart
March 2015

I intently watch the screen as the ultrasound technician at the high-risk obstetrician's office rubs a transducer around my distended abdomen. At 24 weeks pregnant, this is the echocardiogram to check for abnormalities related to lithium exposure in utero. As the sonographer explains the chambers of the heart and blood flow patterns, vague bits of memories return from my previous life as a cardiac nurse. She names off anatomical terms that sound familiar. I listen; there is no reason to mention that I once knew quite a bit about the heart.

After much anticipation, the specialist steps into the room. She watches the screen for a brief time before announcing, "Everything looks perfectly normal. The baby still has a slightly higher than average risk for having a heart murmur, but we will have to wait until he is born. From here on, you can continue visits at your regular obstetrician's office."

After months of praying for a healthy heart, I feel thankful and relieved. There is, however, a lingering bit of worry, as we will have to wait another four months to know the full impact of the medications.

Fear of Judgment
June 2015

I've known enough labor and delivery nurses to know nothing makes them angrier than babies born with drugs in their system; intrauterine drug exposure. Obviously, not mad at the baby but furious with the mom. The sentiment being, "Ruin your own life if you want to, but don't hurt an innocent child."

As I prepare for my delivery, I fear the nurses may put me in that category. I didn't take or do anything illegal, but I know my psychiatric medication can cause withdrawal symptoms in newborns. What are they going to think of me? Are the nurses going to think I am selfish for taking the medication? Are they going to wonder why unstable people like me are allowed to have babies? Are they going to wonder about my ability to love and care for my baby? It is frightening to worry about all the possible judgments.

Pull it together, Leah. You are not the first mother with bipolar. You are a loving mom who knows how to ask for help when necessary. You got this.

Deny, Deny, Deny
July 2015

It's 9:45 a.m. on July 10th, my scheduled induction day. I've sent Tommy and his mother to get breakfast while I get registered in the Labor and Delivery Unit. My Mom stays back with me. The nurse is

165

in the room at the computer, verifying my name and date of birth. She asks, "Any drug allergies?" I peer around my bulging pregnant belly at her, confidently stating, "Nope."

I see Mom frantically digging in her purse. She pulls out a small piece of paper and discretely shows it to me. Mom has written out all the family members' drug allergies. Apparently, she keeps it on her at all times. I see Dad's name with a list of antibiotic allergies. Andrew's name and the drugs he cannot tolerate are also there. Mom is pointing at my name and the list next to it. "Leah's Allergies - Haldol, Lamictal, Depakote."

I look at Mom with big glaring eyes and gritted teeth. My facial expression says, "Hush, I know them. I don't want the nurse to know them." Although puzzled, Mom keeps quiet, sits back down, and tucks away her list.

The nurse finishes with the admission questionnaire by saying, "I will page anesthesia for your epidural."

After the nurse leaves the room, Mom asks, "Why didn't you tell her your allergies?"

"Mom, I've worked in a hospital. They put your drug allergies on everything, including the front of the chart in huge letters. My allergies scream, I am crazy. I've tried so many psych meds that this is only the list of ones I'm allergic to. My OB isn't going to change my psych meds. I just don't want that to be the first thing the staff sees about me."

Mom disagrees. But she doesn't argue either.

Making Hard Choices
July 2015

As I lie in the hospital bed with staff and students whizzing around me, I look down in the surreal moment that only another parent could understand, the moment of meeting my new beautiful baby and staring into his precious eyes. I cry, overwhelmed with emotion. Brand-new baby Cole lets out some short wails as he attempts to acclimate to an unfamiliar world. His little cries are as reassuring as his high APGAR scores. He seems healthy.

After a period of bonding on my chest, a nurse takes Cole to finish his assessment under the warming lamp. I can't help but worry about the possibility of a heart murmur. As the nurse pulls the stethoscope from around her neck and prepares to listen, I ask, "Can you listen to his heart really well? I was on lithium at the start of my pregnancy, so he is at higher risk for a murmur." The nurse cordially agrees. A few moments pass. I watch for clues - any change in her facial expression or body language.

After calmly removing the earpieces from her ears, she informs, "I am really good at hearing murmurs, and he does not have one." She points down to her own pregnant belly. "I've had to take antidepressants my whole pregnancy. I worry too, but you have to take care of yourself. Sometimes you need medication."

There was something monumental in that short conversation, vulnerability leading to validation for both of us. In that brief conversation, all of my fears of "What will the nurses think?" were squashed.

As women, we are not alone in loving our babies deeply, worrying about them, and having to make hard choices. These are universal aspects of motherhood.

After weighing my particular options, I feel that loving my baby well means continuing the single, low-dose medication in order to breastfeed. I fully realize that I may be taking one for the team here. Monotherapy, for me, will likely cause more significant mood swings than the alternative (a cocktail of a few other medications). Still, none of the other drugs are approved for breastfeeding mothers. I, of course, am also not exempt from typical postpartum hormonal difficulties. Even with these factors considered, I still feel the nutritional value of breastfeeding my newborn outweighs my personal costs.

Master of None
September 2015

Against all odds, the university accepts me into the master's program. I start graduate school with a twelve-year-old, six-year-old, and five-week-old. Definitely, the best thing I could have done for my future, but absolutely one of the worst for mood stability.

Now, I am only a couple of weeks into the semester, and I am trying to make it on the lowest medication dose possible despite incredible stress and raging postpartum hormones.

It's been more than a few hours - closer to a full day - of straight sobbing, so I decide to call someone comforting. That someone is Mom. She answers the phone with a sweet "Hello."

I try to get the word "Hello" out, but all I can do is cry. I don't know why this spell has started. I am not okay. As one would expect, I am incredibly stressed out, but this has blindsided me.

As I sob and still haven't said a word, Mom tenderly says, "Leah, I'm on my way over right now. It sounds like you probably want to call Dr. Morris, too." I continue to cry. Mom waits patiently on the phone.

Between sniffles, I finally get out "O - - - K."

There is no end in sight to this sobbing as these tears aren't the healing kind. There's no getting it out and feeling better.

I know I need to do it. Now is the time to call the doctor.

This phone call starts the same way as my call to Mom. The receptionist answers to the sound of my heavy weeping. It takes everything in me to get out, "This is Leah Nash, and I can't stop crying." Somehow, she manages to understand enough to connect me with Dr. Morris.

The doctor explains my options are limited unless I stop breastfeeding. She encourages me to get back on the combination that had worked before my pregnancy.

I continue sobbing while mentally weighing my options as Dr. Morris waits patiently at the other end of the line. This low-dose medication is not enough, and I can't care for myself or anyone else in this state. I have made it as long as I could. I sob and reply, "I don't want to, but I can't... I can't do this any more."

I feel like such a failure. My baby was counting on me, and I let him down because of my bipolar disorder.

At the doctor's recommendation and my own decision, I quit breastfeeding and return to my previous medications. The baby transitions to formula without any trouble while I continue to cry. Not as hard because the medicines are helping, but I still cry plenty. I cry when I make bottles, and I cry when I see people post public service announcements about the benefits of breastfeeding. I feel like such a failure as a mother even though I know he will be okay with formula, and I'm ultimately doing the best thing for not only the two of us but for my whole family.

It is challenging when mental illness makes choices for you. It is incredibly tough when mental illness makes choices for your baby.

With time, it gets a little easier to deal with Cole being a bottle baby. I snuggle him tight as we bond over the inevitable - bottles.

Just Show Up
October 2015

This season of life, maybe life in general is about showing up. I feel stretched far beyond my capabilities but blessed to be given this chance. Often, showing up for me looks like crying the entire way to school, fixing mascara smudges in the parking lot, and walking in as a separate, professional individual. Other times, showing up means serving clients despite my sleepless night, racing heart, and nervous hands.

I aspire for normal but repeatedly settle for just showing up.

{symptoms keep popping up -
bipolar whac-a-mole}

Not-So-Wise Sayings
February 2016

It has been six years since the last ECT treatment. Sometimes I feel I've made tremendous strides that would leave any doctor speechless. At other times, I grow weary and discouraged. What I miss the most is my ability to speak freely - the ability to gain a certain level of mastery of the English language that allows my words to match my thoughts.

Now, an ever-present disconnect remains. My mind knows the ins and outs of a concept, but it takes a conscious effort to conjure up words that match what I'm trying to convey.

Writing is a little less stressful than speaking. There is time to think and pause without being found out. There is time to click and pull up the thesaurus function while in a Word document.

When I started graduate school, I would (and often still do) pick one word out of every sentence to replace with a more eloquent-sounding word; the "thesaurus touch-up." Somehow one word per sentence seemed like the magical number that would make elementary writing sound college level without overdoing it.

However, the simple, everyday use of verbal language stalls me. A constant, internal questioning activates as I speak. *Did I say that right? Is that the word? Did I make a fool of myself by scrambling a wise saying into an idiotic one?*

I share with a friend that my hair doesn't go the direction I want. There is a term for that, but I can't think of it. My mind searches for an alternate word that could work. Nothing. I keep mentally searching, knowing I only have a limited amount of time

173

to come up with something while maintaining the flow of the conversation. I realize I am getting closer. I can feel it. Is it something like "colic"? Thankfully, before I make any attempt, my friend jumps in and says, "Oh, a cowlick." "Yes, a cowlick." I had narrowed it down pretty close on that one. Not bad, but still frustrating.

On another occasion, I thank my sister-in-law for the new rug for our front door, saying, "It really __." I freeze. Is it spruces up or spices up? Or maybe both? Outwardly, I try to laugh it off while asking her what the proper wording is. Internally, I'm furious because it hasn't always been this way.

These stumblings occur multiple times a day. Frequent hesitations and failures with words reinforce my fear of saying something foolish. At times, others will finish my sentences for me. I'm grateful.

I mentally rehearse words others say in an attempt to expand my abilities and patch these verbal holes. I continue to do numerous Internet searches per week on proper grammar.

Mental Health Day
March 2016

My children go to public schools and receive an excellent education, which is fortunate because I can't afford private school. I certainly couldn't handle homeschooling. We barely make it through fifteen minutes of homework together. After school, I function more as a complimentary Internet searcher because I can't figure out what their assignment is; however, I take on a teacher's role for one day a year. The topic is something that I know about - a subject matter that I am more than qualified to teach. Mental Health Day.

Regardless of how in-depth the school curriculum covers mental illness, I still want to discuss it more. No one can function well in the real world without understanding mental illness - whether for oneself, a family member, a friend, a coworker. It is too prevalent to skim over.

Jordan has participated in Mental Health Day with me for a few years. I am still deciding when and how much to tell the younger ones, attempting to maintain the balance of sharing enough but not too much.

As spring emerges, there is typically an accompanying feeling of burnout. With the hints of exhaustion, we take time to care for ourselves and observe this day. Now, there is more to the day than playing hooky. Mental Health Day has a clear and critical message; we go out to lunch anticipating the hard conversations.

The discussion begins by remembering the relatives we have lost to suicide. It is painful to talk about, but in order to change the future, we must not forget the pain of the past.

The statistics are undeniable; Jordan, and my other children, are at an increased risk of having a mental illness. We talk about what to do if mood changes occur. We discuss that thoughts are neither good nor bad... only thoughts, and we can share them even if they become frightening. We rehearse what to do if someone else, such as a friend, is feeling down or suicidal.

As we wrap up the conversation, I ask Jordan if he has any questions for me. He pauses then decides to ask, "Why does bipolar make your memory bad?"

I reply, "Good question. I don't think it's the bipolar itself. My memory became bad with the ECT treatments I had."

He states, "Oh, I just knew you couldn't remember stuff, like the season I played baseball." He chuckles, "But that's okay. We were terrible and never won a game."

You can almost see the gears turning as he quietly processes and asks, "What do they do with those treatments?"

In an attempt to be child-friendly, I reply, "It's kind of like a seizure that the doctor creates to help the brain."

I realize he was too little and never knew about the ECT. This entire time, I assumed he understood about ECT because he was aware of my memory troubles.

This is the exact reason we have these days - to share and clarify misconceptions. I am thankful for these talks and hopeful they will transform our family's legacy.

Crippling Panic
April 2016

I wake up and instantly recognize this all too familiar feeling. My nighttime medications and a good night's rest were not enough to reset the panic button. I swing my legs over the side of the bed. My body is telling me to stay put. Nothing is okay, not in this moment, not on this day, probably never. I make myself a cup of coffee, which will have to be the only caffeine for the day if I want any chance at beating this anxiety. Seeking calm, I turn on the essential oil diffuser.

Cole wakes up. He is at the stage where he knows what he wants but can't say it, often resorting to other means of communication - scratching, biting, and flailing on the floor, which does nothing to help my anxiety. Everything in me wants to throw a fit too, but I have to hold this together.

I'm feeling worse. My cheeks and arms are now numb. I feel like my insides are bigger than my skin, crawling out. How am I going to make it through this day? How am I going to make it through the next two minutes?

My world is closing in. The sounds are getting louder. The house is getting smaller. I want to run and hide. I don't know what else to do. I pop an "as needed" medication for anxiety.

Next, Micah wakes up. It's been two hours since the medication, and I can't tell any difference. I feel like a failure. Why can't I handle life? Tons of parents work full-time jobs and take care of their kids. I can't even make it to breakfast. I feel discouraged.

It is also Tuesday, the day Micah goes with his Dad. I try to treasure every moment before I take him. As we are walking to the car, he says, "I'm sorry if I've been too much to handle."

My heart sinks. Oh no. Even though my best attempt to conceal my misery, Micah has noticed. Noticed and blamed himself.

"It's not you, buddy. My anxiety has just been really bad."

He says, "Oh yeah, your medicine thing."

"Yes, my medicine thing. Not you."

He quickly bounces back to his chipper self and decides it is necessary to practice every song in his school play as we're in the car. My anxiety is still unbearably high. He cycles through the National

Anthem to a song about remembering the veterans to "This Land is Your Land."

Everything in me is screaming. Run. Find dark and quiet. Close all the curtains and get in bed. Snuggle up under a weighted blanket until this is over.

I fight to listen to Micah's songs. It isn't his singing or the topics. It's the over-stimulation at a time of panic. While driving through the neighborhood, I take a deep breath, and a tear falls behind my sunglasses.

After what seems like an eternity, but couldn't have been more than five minutes, Micah concludes his last song. I quickly ask myself, still internally panicked with my heart racing, *What would a normal mom do right now?* I force a smile hoping the words of encouragement will sound more sincere. "You did a great job." I don't dare turn around for fear he will see the tears running down my cheek. It is all too much. Anything but silence and darkness is too much.

Dear Future Self
May 2016

Because of my mood disorder, it is inevitable that, at some point, there will be bad days again. But right now, I'm on a streak of feeling good, feeling balanced. Regulated days are the time to prepare for the difficult days. I've written a letter to my future self, for when the darkness creeps in and leaves me sobbing and suicidal.

Dear Future Struggling Self,

If you're reading this, it has gotten worse again. It all feels dark and hopeless. You feel like it will last forever.

I knew you'd say that, so I'm writing to remind you of today - one of the better days you will forget about when your mood changes.

It was a pretty typical day, but there was joy throughout. You got hugs from the kids. You laughed with friends until tears ran down your face. It was nice enough outside to sit on the patio in short sleeves. The sun was peeking out from behind the scattered clouds. You made a resident in the nursing home smile as you joked and danced together. You were thankful to be here, on this earth, for these moments. And joyful moments like these will come again at some point.

The key is not to lose hope. Even when hope dwindles, it is still present. Although this emotional pain feels like it will last an eternity, it is not permanent. Take comfort that the feelings associated with this depression are real but not in control.

Now, practice some self-care and be kind to yourself.

Stay hopeful,
Me

Treacherous Transitions
June 2016

Tommy and I have been planning this move for months. I prepare myself. Leah, it's only five miles down the road. We have a month of double rent, so there's no hurry at all. Slow and steady. I remind myself of this over and over. I know what I usually do with moves - harness manic energy and go for days without sleep until it is done. Between graduate school and little Cole, I have to find a better, more stable plan. I pack a couple of boxes a day, make a point to ask for help, and try to ignore the chaos.

I always chuckle when doctors ask if stressors could be contributing to my mood instability. I think Dr. Morris has given up on this question. Even without the move, I continually have three pediatric stressors, which don't even count outside sources. Change and stress are my enemies, or as Dr. Morris calls it, "my kryptonite."

My moving plan fails miserably. I didn't expect this transition to be as tricky as it has been. I guess eleven-month-olds are drawn to boxes and feel the need to scatter everything. Cole undoes everything I try to finish. But, it isn't just him. It's me. As much as I wish it weren't so, I do not handle change well. I crave order. Order represents stability.

I can prepare, organize, and get things done quickly. Mom often tells me, "You get more done in one day than anyone I know." But now, I'm physically drained. Mentally, I should be slowing down as well, but the ideas start relentlessly pouring in.

Localization of (Improbable) Sounds
June 2016

We have been in the new house for almost two weeks. Things are coming together nicely, including the new sectional for the living room, rug for the bonus room, and cushions for the patio chairs. I have even finished my quirky organizational preferences, such as arranging my closet by color and alphabetizing spices. When everything around me feels chaotic, these techniques provide the illusion of control.

However, it does not seem to matter how much I accomplish; my mind races faster, telling me to do more. The racing thoughts are so loud my ears begin to ring.

It seems highly problematic that there are pinecones in the side yard. I no longer like the arrangement of the furniture. I must repaint the mailbox right this instant. I know where this is headed, and I try to intervene. *Leah, you don't have to do all these things right now. It is eleven o'clock, time to get some rest.* Rational mind triumphs and I decide to get ready for bed.

I step into the bathroom. It stands in the same condition as when the house was built in 1962, complete with rose-colored tile and an unused heating vent on the far wall. I turn on the water, giving it time to heat up as I undress.

The music turns on as well - the same four tones. They repeat, almost like the ringing of a cell phone.

That's strange. The neighbors must be listening to music. I put my head to the bathroom window, but it doesn't seem to be coming from there. I look down and see the vent below. It sounds like it is coming from that direction. The shower water pours down in the background as I place my head to the metal grate covering the vent, but that isn't it. I stand up and turn around. Oh, it sounds like it is coming from the hallway door. The same four tones continue. I take two steps to the left and stop.

After a few minutes of searching the bathroom, it hits me. My mind flashes back to an audiology class and the lecture on sound localization. No matter what direction I turn, it doesn't get any louder or softer.

Panic sets in, and I freeze. *Oh my God. I am hearing things that are not real.* After a few minutes, I robotically step into the shower. The hot water pours down my head as I begin sobbing. *This is it. I have completely lost it. Is my diagnosis progressing? How do I even tell anyone?* I cry until the hot water runs out and turns cold.

After turning off the shower, I notice the tones have finally disappeared, but the drain gurgles louder than usual as the last few drops of water go down the pipe. As I walk down the hallway, the sound of my wet feet on the hardwood seems more pronounced than usual. There seems to be a heightened sensitivity of my hearing following the beeping noises. I walk into the bedroom, and the fan is obnoxiously loud. I quickly turn it off.

I'm afraid it is too late to call the doctor for this non-life-threatening emergency. I can't deal with this on my own. I am terrified and need to talk to someone to process. I call Camila. She has the highest tolerance for shocking news and can handle just about anything.

After sobbing through my explanation of the events, Camila says in a soothing voice, "That must have been frightening."

I blurt out all of my fears that I have something new that is now wrong with me - something worse than ever. I am losing touch with reality and going permanently insane.

Camila listens and validates my fears. In the kindest way possible, she says, "Leah, you probably don't remember it, but this isn't the first time you have heard or seen things that weren't there. I do think it is your bipolar." She continues to tell me how I saw bugs crawling and heard sirens while initially trying to get stabilized.

Strangely, this was the most reassuring thing she could have told me. It has gotten this bad before, and it didn't progress to anything worse. Until now, I had never thought of it, but my diagnosis includes with psychotic features. Why didn't I think to ask about that?

As we finish the conversation, Camila makes sure I'm okay until the morning when I will call the doctor. She was calm, which made me feel a tiny bit better, or at least as good as I could under the circumstances. There aren't many friends one can tell about having auditory hallucinations. I don't know what I would do without her.

I Will Not Be Referring to Myself As "Crazy" Anymore
June 2016

Once again, the office staff has graciously squeezed me into Dr. Morris' schedule. I remain terrified by the noises I heard last night and feel the urgent need to get her opinion.

Dr. Morris calls me back from the waiting room. I sit down on the sofa in her office. I feel ridiculous in my navy blue scrubs required for school clinicals. From the outside, it appears as though I could save a life at any moment, but inside I'm a complete mess struggling to keep myself together.

She asks, "What's going on?"

I blurt out, "Isn't it ironic? I'm wearing scrubs because I have to go to a nursing home and do assessments. I can't give any type of assessment when I'm hearing stuff. I'm the one who is crazy."

Dr. Morris is usually pretty easygoing, but she sternly stops me this time. "Do not say you are crazy. You have a medical condition just like someone with diabetes or high blood pressure." I'm taken aback. I fully expected her to agree I've lost it and am in no condition to do anything, especially not an assessment of someone else.

She encourages me, reminding me that I have something to offer to the medical field. Dr. Morris continues, "There are individuals who treat psychology as inferior to other areas in the medical field, but psychology is backed with research in the same way." I learn that referring to myself as "crazy" takes away from the years of progress in the medical field.

After a stern talkin' to, we go on to discuss symptoms, and she conveys the need for an increase in medication dosage. Dr. Morris seems much less alarmed by the auditory hallucinations than I was. She even comments, "Oh, it only lasted for a few minutes."

I don't know precisely how Dr. Morris did it, but I walk out of her office feeling empowered. The panic associated with the auditory hallucinations dwindles as courage rises. I can represent the study of psychology well; I have something to give. I vow never to refer to myself as "crazy" again. Lesson learned.

Greatest Weakness, Greatest Strength
August 2016

A few years ago, we rescued this mutt (or hybrid, depending on who you ask). Our rescue dog, Milo, started in a puppy mill before going to an extremely busy family who left him neglected. There was always an understanding that Milo had separation anxiety but never an official diagnosis. He had been doing pretty well until Cole came along, and now, the move has completely pushed the poor creature over the edge. All of his progress is gone. He is having accidents in the house, panicking to the point of vomiting, and attempting to destroy anything (doors, crate, etc.) that separates us.

I can't take it anymore. Milo is not happy, and I'm certainly not happy either. We go to the veterinarian, where I explain Milo's worsening symptoms. After listening patiently and asking some additional questions, the veterinarian confirms what I already knew. Milo has a mental illness. The vet says, "I don't know if you know anyone with mental illness, but sometimes it takes a while to find a medication combination that works." I tip my head to the right ever so slightly and silently nod, enough to imply I understand what he is saying but not enough to broadcast I know someone, and it's ME!

I can't help but chuckle internally. As a kid, I loved the movie "101 Dalmatians," especially the scene where the dogs look like their owners. I don't have tan curly poodle hair, but maybe this dog is more like me than I thought.

My second thought gets a little deeper. I think back to a Psychology of Personality class I took where we learned that our greatest weakness could also be our greatest strength. It is so simple to see in a dog. Milo's separation anxiety can make his life miserable and get him into a great deal of trouble; however, this same weakness is precisely what makes him so sweet to people, even rowdy children. I can't even begin to count how many people have said, "He is so good with the kids" or "I don't know why he puts up with the kids, but he is amazing." This dog is extraordinarily gentle and tolerant. I wholeheartedly believe his separation anxiety, his greatest weakness, makes him so loving and patient. Out of his weakness emerges his greatest strength.

Why couldn't I see it in myself? This entire time, I have thought of my bipolar solely as a weakness. Not like a personal failure weakness, just a weakness in a negative sense. I begin to think of the great strengths that also come from this painful illness. It is much harder to see in myself than a dog, but they are there.

I have learned to handle honest answers and to genuinely ask the question, "How are you?" I am not afraid to sit in discomfort. I realize cliché words and shallow attempts of encouragement don't fix anything. I am learning to be thankful. After losing my mind and talents, I am filled with gratitude instead of arrogance when I successfully complete a task. I chuckle, thinking of what this mentally ill mutt has shown me.

Opposing Forces
October 2016

I've heard of neurological conditions that cause opposing muscle groups to contract simultaneously, causing severe pain. I feel the psychological version of this is a mixed episode, where mania and depression compete simultaneously, causing severe mental distress.

This episode started with anxiety. I know why, the unusually high-stress level - but it was unavoidable this week. It is midterms. Tommy is in Canada for a wedding. I have three kiddos, a ton of work, and little help. It doesn't take much to throw off my routine and stability. I make it for the first few days. I compensate for the lack of childcare by going full speed until the wee hours of the night.

The rational part of my brain nags, *Leah, you're accelerating. You know you can't maintain this speed for long.* I appreciate recognizing the signs early so that I can intervene. My outcomes have proven to be much more positive with early intervention.

I pause to think about what would be helpful at this moment. Many stress-relieving options are out of the question because I am chasing a toddler around the house. I do the best I can. I load him in the stroller, and we go for a brisk walk.

I am keenly aware of the current mental tug-of-war.

There is a stimulating aspect of the episode; my heart is pounding, and I feel like I could run for miles. My legs are in physical pain from the last few days of constantly moving (cleaning, rearranging, yard work, etc.) My thoughts are racing, and I feel that familiar sense of urgency about everything.

The depressant aspect is also struggling for control. I wish I could sleep. Completing everything that felt like it had to be done instantly has left me exhausted. Depression leaves me feeling fat, unattractive, and worthless. I alternate between not eating and binge-eating carbs.

I don't have the enjoyment associated with pure mania. This episode is psychologically uncomfortable. Part of my mind signals to go faster while the other part is screeching all mental activity to a halt. My mind's racing ideas fire rapidly, yet I am too physically exhausted to complete a thought. I begin to leave off the ends of sentences, too drained to compute what those last few words should be. I chuckle and say, "Sorry. When I get tired, I don't finish my sentences." Internally, I'm not chuckling, though. My self-monitoring conscience whispers, *There's another red flag. You need to come up with a plan quickly.*

The plan looks like a combination of medication adjustments, intentional self-care, and - despite all desires for independence - asking for help from my parents.

Perpetual Panic
November 2016

Typically, my anxiety will last a day, maybe two, max. This episode is more persistent. It has been over a week of feeling stuck in a perpetual panic. My irritability is increasing with time. Anxiety fuels the feeling of impending doom. I mentally negotiate all the activities I can cancel.

Unfortunately, there will be negative consequences if I don't show up for practicum. Just be present. Anything is better than lying in bed earning a zero.

These are the big things that require me to show up.

I also struggle to do the basic, everyday tasks. Even something as simple as checking my emails seems like an insurmountable chore. Anxiety whispers, something terrible is coming, and it could come at any time. I hesitate to respond to any contact. I look at my phone and see there is a new email. It takes hours before I muster the courage to check the sender's name. When it is junk mail, I delete it with the feeling I'm on borrowed time.

Inevitably, I get an email that requires me to read it and respond.

I fear the sender will either be writing to tell me bad news or ask me to do something. I can't handle bad news right now, and I definitely can't do anything beyond basic survival. I focus on breathing and staying grounded. That is it. Schedule full.

I see a new email. Crap. This email is from a professor at school. Rationally, I know it is probably the final review of a diagnostic report I submitted. Still, it is frightening, and I immediately close the email. With this level of paralyzing anxiety, I am currently unable to communicate with the outside world.

I hide out for a couple more days until the episode passes.

Conforming

December 2016

We have been in the new neighborhood for about six months. Somehow, I've managed to contain my instability within the walls of our house. Tommy and the kids have seen the mood swings but neighbors have not. The worst thing the neighbors may have noticed is that I am still in my pajamas when I take the dog out at noon or the days where I do enormous amounts of yard work (mania disguised as a responsible member of the homeowners' association). So far, there haven't been any ambulances taking me to the hospital or anything else to cause a scene here. I haven't blown my fresh start at being normal.

A combination of feelings and a myriad of questions circle within me when I am well enough to hide my bipolar. I feel torn. I don't want to share my history, but even if I did, I still don't feel like I would even know where to start.

The whisper of shame sets in. *Keep your mouth shut. They won't understand. Nobody else is as crazy as you. You will never be trusted. You will be excluded from social functions. Parents won't allow any more play dates with their children. Don't ever let anyone see the true you.*

But I value authenticity more than just about anything. I don't want to live as an imposter. I don't want to trade authenticity for the hope of gaining some stranger's approval.

I rehearse possible conversation starters in my head. *How could I share a little bit but not too much? Who would be a good neighbor for a test run? Maybe I could substitute the word depression for bipolar to lessen the blow.* I could twist and contort my words in many different ways, but none of these explanations feel authentic.

When I do use the word "bipolar," people are often bewildered. Reactions have included, "but you are so calm" and "I can't imagine you having a temper and throwing stuff." There seems to be a preconceived notion about the personality and behaviors of an individual with bipolar. I'd love to shatter this misconception, but I struggle to know when or how much to share.

All of this questioning and rehearsing in my head while remaining outwardly silent leads me to feel like an imposter. Am I a mentally ill person posing as a suburban mom? Am I a suburban mother who purposefully conceals her mental illness? I wonder how to be appropriately vulnerable and honest.

If I were to be honest, first I would need to know who I truly am. Sometimes, I sit around thinking about the lines of demarcation, the exact starting and stopping points of bipolar intertwined with my being. The more I think, the more I realize I am not even sure where the lines of "me" blur with the beginning of bipolar. I have spent the majority, if not all of my adult life, on the spectrum of bipolar.

It is easy to tell the drastic influences at each end of mania and depression. But from there, it gets a little murky. Am I genuinely confident and outgoing, or is that a touch of hypomania? Am I the true me when I am a quiet introvert who likes to recharge alone, or is it possibly a hint of depression? Am I an exercise fanatic or a content couch potato? Am I a night owl or an over sleeper? I am not sure.

Maybe the answer is D. All the above.

Everyone has "off days" when they don't feel like themselves. The problem is after so many "off days," I have lost touch with what a typical day looks like. I am all these things in varying degrees at various times. There are so many facets that it is difficult to know where the true center - the true "me" - lies.

If I were asked to hit a buzzer when I get to the authentic Leah without any mood changes, I wouldn't know when to buzz. After all the mood swings and facades and trying to be normal, I seem to have lost touch with what exact stopping point constitutes the actual Leah.

I wonder who I am, who I was, who I am pretending to be, and who I wish I were.

Disaster Relief
January 2017

My moods are cycling so fast all I can do is attempt damage control. Keep the relational losses and pain to a minimum.

I know what started this cycle - working a little side gig 9 out of 10 consecutive days. As much as I want to do what others can do, I can't. I can only hold it together for so long before I mentally unravel. This time, two days of nonstop deep cleaning, including sorting out 14 bags of clothing to donate to the thrift store, demonstrate the instability. I inform Tommy and the kids, "We are only keeping items that bring us joy. We are going to live a minimalist lifestyle."

Next comes labeling the kitchen cabinets and getting rid of gluten, dairy, corn, sugar, preservatives, additives, or food color.

Abruptly and compulsively, I declare, "We are decreasing inflammation in the gut and eliminating neurotoxins."

These extreme changes quickly morph into lethargy and extreme irritability.

This time I almost lost my temper at work. I got chewed out for being two minutes late. Two. If they only knew, my problems are so much bigger than two minutes right now. I keep to myself and (barely) successfully finish my shift without expressing my irritability and rage.

Homelife isn't so lucky. The ones I love end up taking the brunt of the instability. After snapping at every family member, I burst into tears. "I can't take it anymore. I need a break. It is all too much." I drag my feet, exhausted, crying with my head hung low, as I shuffle to bed.

It's no use. I wake up to my hands nervously shaking. Now the anxiety is high in addition to the other symptoms. I scrub the kitchen floor on my knees, although we own a mop. While pacing around the house, I attempt to chase all the racing trains of thoughts, each jumbling into the last.

Ahhh, enough!

I, possibly impulsively or maybe necessarily, quit the part-time job. Thankfully, my family expresses their full support. It isn't worth all of this instability for the tiny paychecks.

Just because I quit the job doesn't mean all the symptoms subside. I pause to make a mental note of all the lingering difficulties, and there are a bunch. I need to move up my appointment with the psychiatrist.

What will Dr. Morris say?

This episode seems to have characteristics of mania, anxiety, and depression. I wonder if it is rapid cycling or a mixed episode. Either way, I hope for relief, especially for those around me.

I think it is easier for the kids to understand and steer clear. Tommy, on the other hand, takes it personally. He ends up feeling helpless. Tommy lists everything he does for the family - ultimately trying to defend his case.

He, like me, longs for a break.

Tommy shares, "You're a lot to deal with. One moment you are cleaning. The next, you are a gluten free vegan and can't eat all these things. Then, you say you do all the work around here and nothing is good enough. It's been five years of this, and it's a lot."

Today's Therapy Spotlight Is On Me
February 2017

Tommy and I have started couples' counseling. It's hard blending a family and raising kids. The focus of today's session is drifting away from parenting and onto my mood swings. Tommy and I have both been under quite a bit of stress, exacerbating my symptoms. I am past the point of faking regulation.

Tommy reiterates the conversations we have been having. Looking down the sofa and directly at me, he shares, "It's harder to live with you than you know. Your moods are all over the place. I never know what I am going to walk into when I get home from work. I have to be strong for you, but your emotions take priority over mine."

It's hard to hear. I've never considered the uncertainty Tommy must feel on his drive home from work. I also struggle to think about the pain he must feel, not to have his emotions valued in the way he needs.

I hate it when I get snippy and say things I will soon regret. However, I don't want him to bring up bipolar in the middle of an argument (even when there is an apparent influence) for fear of feeling invalidated.

In highly dysregulated states, my focus narrows and prevents the processing of anything else. Subsequently, his emotions, along with all other emotionally taxing input, are disregarded.

I leave the session feeling discouraged. How does one come up with a solution to this? The bipolar symptoms may ebb and flow, but they aren't going away. As I replay his complaints, a tiny voice questions, *Can he put up with this for the long haul? Could anyone?*

Tremors: An Unwelcome Reminder of Frailty
March 2017

I sit down at the kitchen table to type a research article critique, one of many assignments due this week. Documents are scattered everywhere, surrounding my laptop. I place my wrists on the computer and begin to type. Suddenly, two fingers, my ring and pinky fingers, start shaking uncontrollably. The tremors are easily visible to the naked eye. I attempt to continue working by utilizing the two-finger pecking method. Too frightened and frustrated to continue, I give up on the assignment for the night.

Dr. Morris believes this is likely a side effect of a medication started last week. I am disappointed because I was beginning to notice an improvement in my mood. Out of necessity, Dr. Morris discontinues the drug, and thankfully, the tremors resolve.

This incident is another reminder of my frailty. When all is well and stable, my natural tendency is to believe I have power over every aspect of my mental illness. This belief leads to significant disappointment and shock when instability or side effects creep up.

The flipside would be to believe I have no control - to do as I wish with no regard to my mental state. A "what will be will be" mantra. I cannot give in to this way of thinking either, as I see the correlation between my choices and more extended periods of stability.

So, how does one balance the reality that my choices (self-care, rest, being positive) can impact - either positively or negatively - the number of "good days." Meanwhile, also knowing that, while I am not a victim, the reality of being an individual with bipolar has aspects that I have no control over regardless of my good choices or the previous success of my current mediation cocktail. It is difficult to fight for the future while admitting, in all likelihood, mental illness may still take certain aspects away.

Because of bipolar, I feel there will always be some degree of uncertainty about the future. Mental illness is far more dominant than I wish. Perhaps this is the realization: I have less control than I would care to admit. Maybe this is true for most people, but they are just able to masquerade under the guise of stability better than I can at this point.

Can You Define "Normal" Because I Think I'm Getting Close
April 2017

I am noticing an overall trend of more "normal" days. Let's be clear; I don't have a firm grasp of what "normal" truly means.

For me, I feel like a typical functioning adult when... I'm not too drugged to get my kids to the bus stop by 7:45 a.m. I get a little excited when I match a new outfit from my closet instead of staying in pajamas for days. I can listen to my body's hunger signals without ravenously destroying numerous servings of sweets for breakfast. I feel up to returning phone calls and emails. I can listen attentively without struggling to suppress racing thoughts. My mind is clear enough to read and retain information. I am disciplined enough to make it to the gym but balanced enough to sense when to stop.

I can stick up for my needs without feeling too insecure about speaking up. I am confident that those around me hear what I hear. I can let the small things go instead of looking for my opportunity to mouth off. I can feel the troubles of the day without being too sedated to care or too labile to handle it. I am balanced when I daydream of ways to help others instead of focusing on feelings of impending doom. I can make it to the afternoon without relying on caffeine or requiring multiple naps. I can go to the store without feeling like people are staring at me, judging me, and supernaturally knowing my psychiatric history.

These things make a good, normal day.

I know these good days are sprinkled (and sometimes plastered) with hard days in between. It is tempting to feel that the hard days are steps backward and nothing more than progress lost, but I slowly see a difference. The terrible days are now fewer and farther between, and I am starting to sense when they are coming. I frequently ask my psychiatrist about warning signs and symptoms.

I now know there are things I can't get away with if I want to remain stable. I absolutely cannot handle extreme stress, missed sleep, or excessive alcohol. It is worth saying "no" in exchange for lower anxiety levels. It is worth missing a few events to recharge with a warm bath and an early bedtime.

I am encouraged by the streaks of normalcy.

Live For Success
April 2017

I think about the future - what it might hold, my capabilities, and how to make the most of the cards I've been dealt. I pick up a library book with words of wisdom from a famous entrepreneur. One page, in particular, catches my attention as the author mentions Ralph Waldo Emerson's quote, "Hitch your wagon to a star."

Idioms are still tricky for me, often confusing and challenging to remember correctly, but this one stands out. My mind quickly wanders away from lofty goals and levels of achievement to the word "hitch."

What is my soul hitched to?

Fallacies I've come to believe over the years rapidly pop up.

You're visibly crazy. Your reality is flawed. You will never get off of disability. You are inadequate, and others will find out. The kids will suffer because of having a mother with bipolar.

I look at my future through these jaded, twisted beliefs. It is dark and stifled. Though there may be tiny bits of truth that are undeniable, focusing on and "hitching" to these will not take me star-ward.

When going for an interview, we hear it said, "Dress for success." What if I were to live for success? How would that look? I start thinking of things that could help me be the best version of myself.

I purposefully and uncomfortably place myself in professional environments, absorbing wording, mannerisms, and skills.

I start delegating a little more, asking Tommy and the kids for help, so I can invest time in bettering myself.

I listen to hours of various self-improvement trainings on everything from self-esteem to social skills to handling rejection. With each video, my confidence increases slightly. I learn to listen a little better to others. I feel more capable of being a competent conversationalist.

I read books on addressing fears.

When talking about my anxiety, depression, etc., I learn to swap "I am" statements with "I have." I have bipolar, but it is not all that I am. My entire being does not revolve around my psychiatric condition. Therefore, I will not say, 'I am bipolar.'

I care for my body as it is the vessel to reach my goals. Despite cravings, I do my best to eat well. Despite exhaustion and lethargy, I attempt to exercise consistently.

I don't know the next steps to "live for success" and ultimately reach my highest altitude, but I have to believe my options will be greater if I make plans and focus on more positive beliefs.

{glimmer of insight}

The Egg Drop Experiment
May 2017

I think I've begun unfolding the mystery of why the mere thought of God makes me cry.

Like catching up with a childhood friend, you can easily pick up where you left off. More than that, it's the understanding that comes from looking into that old friend's eyes when you are not okay. You don't have to say a word because they already know. With that full acceptance comes the freedom to cry.

That's how this relationship with God feels. I don't have to worry about putting how hard it's been into words. There is no need for detail; He has witnessed it all. I can cry in His comforting presence.

For years I've worried God might not be as good as I'd hoped He would be, that He wouldn't live up to my expectations. All the struggles and disappointments of the past would seemingly support that belief.

Ironically, it is quite the opposite. The more I've struggled, the more firmly I have come to believe God far exceeds any expectation I'd ever had. While I was busy worrying if He was good enough, God was working horrible circumstances for my good.

I don't know why I had to lose what feels like so much or continue going through these struggles. I don't understand why God has allowed it, but looking back, I can see He has provided during every moment.

My mind thinks back to a project we did in middle school. The teacher told us that each of us must drop an egg off the top row of the bleachers. It was our job to make sure the egg landed in one piece. Our class rummaged through bins of supplies, pulling out pieces of foam and bubble wrap. We prepared that egg for the fall, wrapping and taping and adding as many layers of protection as possible.

As soon as my hand released the padded egg, I turned and sprinted down the bleachers to the point directly below where I had dropped the egg. As I peeled back the layers upon layers of padding and tape, I carefully inspected all the sides of the shell. Not a crack.

As strange as it sounds, I feel like the egg. Through the desperation of terrible loss, I didn't notice the layers of padding God had wrapped me in. Though, I still don't know why I had to go through what felt like years of free-falling.

In retrospect, that period comprised the most graceful way to hit rock bottom. The timing was impeccable on so many occasions. If my work hadn't been concerned enough to call when I didn't show up, I might not have made it. If I didn't get my current doctor, I might not have realized other treatment options. If I didn't get introduced to my DBT therapist, I likely would have continued with a level of emotional instability that was too great for any medication to curtail. If a caseworker didn't give me information, graduate school wouldn't have been an option. If a friend hadn't connected us with a local charity, the kids wouldn't have had food or Christmas presents. I know of so many instances, and certainly there are more I do not.

It has taken years to realize, but I am starting to get a glimpse of the perfect provision and incredible growth that could not have occurred any other way. It is this trust that allows me to continue on an often-difficult journey - to hope when it seems foolish.

Heart Work, Artwork
May 2017

Micah is in counseling (and has been since the divorce). As hard as it was for me, as an adult, to process everything with his father, he has to try to make sense of it as an eight-year-old. Quite the task.

Every once in a while, Micah will get a homework assignment from his counselor. This week the task is pretty simple and focuses on identifying feelings. His therapist has drawn a large heart on a blank piece of paper. Micah is to color the heart with the emotions he is experiencing - coloring more of the heart for stronger feelings and using a different color for each one.

After a couple of minutes, Micah gets up from the kitchen table to ask for help. He is stumped. After four "regular" feelings, he is out of options.

Oh, I can so relate! I'm ecstatic! "Can I show you something?"

He is not quite sure where this is going, but in need of help, he agrees.

"Remember the color wheel in art class? Well, there is one like that for feelings." I go to the computer, pull up a DBT feelings wheel, and hit print.

As I hand it to him, he looks down at the page. His eyes light up with surprise.

"What? There are this many feelings?"

You know when you have those rare and fleeting moments when you feel like 'I'm awesome at this parenting thing'? That's exactly how this moment feels. I think I did something right! I didn't know anything about emotions at Micah's age. I get a glimpse that my pain does have some purpose. Maybe, my hard work will change the course of the family's future - a new generation of more emotionally literate people.

Micah finishes coloring his heart. Fourteen feelings all balled up into one sweet eight-year-old heart.

Perfection Does Not Need Accommodations
May 2017

After years of perceived failure, I keep hoping to reach a point of feeling as though I am enough. Trying to get to the elusive finish line of success is exhausting. Initially, the goal started with, if I could just take care of the kids and keep the house tidy, I would be successful. That morphed into, if I can just do graduate school while keeping up my other responsibilities, I can be proud of myself. Next, I think, if I can just hold down a job and be successful (aka perfect) at work, I will have value.

Through the course of this disorder, I've lost many of the things I used to determine my value. What is left is a world of trying to find new things I can cling to and am capable of. My children, continually calculating thier latest mischief, seem to have made it their life mission to make sure I never feel competent as a mother.

The focus of the past five years has been to push through bipolar, to overcompensate for insecurities by being stronger and working harder. What if I were to stop striving so hard, maybe give 90% instead of 110%?

I've been given accommodations by everyone (the government, my doctors, school, family, and friends). Everyone except me. I don't want accommodations; I want to be perfect.

As I'm thinking this, I look down at Cole, toddling around the kitchen floor. He has grown an incredible amount over the past year and a half, but his value has not changed. Even though he is an emotionally volatile toddler, his importance has not and cannot change.

Changing the finish line to attempt to obtain value is like saying, "Cole will have value when he can write his name. Once he can do simple addition, he will be worthy. Or even, once he stops putting army guys in the toilet, writing on the walls, and digging through the trash can, he will be enough." I'd never say these things to him, but in a roundabout way, I'm telling them to myself.

What if I were to honestly believe I am enough and have value just as I am right now? I have the same amount of value I did at the peak of my career and the depth of my depression. Once I fully believe that accolades do not drive my worth, maybe then I will be free to slow down the pace to grow at a healthy rate.

"I Think It Was The Devil."
June 2017

Last night, we went to dinner with a couple from our old church. About halfway into the evening, the wife, Ashley, leaned over to share that her sister is going through a rough time. She told of her

207

sister's bizarre behaviors, heartbreaking struggles, hospitalization, and medication trials through her new diagnosis of bipolar.

Ashley looked at me and asked, "I know you have been through stuff, and I don't know the details. Is this what it was like for you? I have never seen anything like it. She looked like she was demon possessed, talking to stuff that wasn't there."

I said a quick prayer in my head. Please let me respond in love and truthfulness. Church people with inadequate knowledge can be dangerous. It is always frightening to be vulnerable, but I also saw the concern and confusion on her face. I divulged that I, like her sister, have been hospitalized with bipolar while struggling to find the proper medications.

Ashley asked, "How long were you in the hospital?"

I hesitantly replied, "Actually, I've been hospitalized a lot of times. Fourteen times for different lengths of time from a few days to a few weeks."

She abruptly asked, "Do you see stuff that isn't there like her? I think it was the devil, and I took her to church so they could pray for her. Then, we got kicked out of church because she wouldn't stop screaming."

I took a deep breath and internally scanned for anger welling up within me. Mixing spiritual beliefs with psychiatric illness has been an emotionally triggering, disheartening subject for me. This time, instead of anger, I was filled with deep sadness and disappointment that church members, who are supposed to be an example of how to love well, would turn away a hurting person.

I didn't even know where to start, but I calmly explained, "I do have hallucinations sometimes. And I have thought I had super powers like knowing where all the police are so I can speed down the interstate going over 100 mph. Lots of things can go with bipolar and it doesn't have to be demons. As far as the spiritual aspect, I have prayed and prayed for God to take it away, but He hasn't. For some reason, I still have it and am learning and growing through it."

She continued to ask more questions, specifically about my medications. I shared my current concoction with the caveat, "Everyone is different and it can be hard to find something that works well enough without over-sedating."

At the end of the conversation, Ashley thanked me, saying, "I don't know anyone else who has been through this who I could talk to" and the conversation quickly shifted to a lighter topic.

I keep thinking about that conversation. At times in the past, I have been deeply offended when people have implied bipolar is related to spiritual warfare. Why didn't I have the same reaction with Ashley? It has been so easy to feel judged in the Bible belt. There are many well-meaning religious individuals who will link mental illness to a lack of faith. These suggestions have had devastating effects on my faith and self-esteem in the past. I have even heard of churches telling their members to get off of medications leading to deadly consequences.

But this conversation feels different. I can appreciate Ashley's questions and comments for what they are: Her search for truth.

Personally, I have come to a peace in my faith that God undoubtedly does have the power to heal me, yet for reasons unbeknownst to me, He has not. I don't know why He has allowed the ravages of bipolar, but I certainly don't believe it is because of dark powers at work within me. I don't know why some individuals quickly attribute bipolar to a lack of spirituality, but attribute other diseases like hypertension, diabetes, and cancer to physiological factors.

The Creator of the universe and the Maker of my neurochemistry knows the dysfunction down to the cellular level. Currently, He provides for me through highly qualified doctors, medications, and insight into ways to promote self-regulation.

These truths have solidified in my soul; the questioning and spiritual journeys of others no longer feel threatening. Instead of feeling insulted, I feel honored she felt secure enough to come to me with the hard questions and allowed for conversation despite a typically isolating illness.

Recall the Letter
June 2017

It has been a year since I wrote the letter to myself. For the first time since prophylactically writing, I need the letter. The severity and speed of my mood changes catches me off-guard.

I'm walking down the hospital hallway for clinical orientation. I am to be the provider, not the patient. My eyes feel like a dam holding back tears that could burst forth at any moment. My motivation and attention have dwindled. I feel apathetic and just plain blah.

A tiny thought intrudes. Life is too hard. You can't keep doing this. It would be so much easier if it were all over - if you weren't here anymore.

I startle myself. It has been years since a thought like this has crept in. Almost every hospitalization was for some type of progression of this train of thought.

Life was equally as hard a week ago and a month ago, but I was thankful to be here. Something has changed, and I know it's my thought process. I'm immediately fearful of an acute meltdown, one as intense as they have been in the past. I must counter this thought.

Leah, what did your letter say? Try to remember as much of the letter as you can. I think back. *The sun is shining, and you made someone laugh today. This feeling won't last forever.* That's it! I do remember that part about this feeling won't last forever.

That line brings comfort and a bit of hope. This state is temporary. It has gotten this bad (even worse), and I've still emerged victorious. For now, I call Dr. Morris for worsening depression symptoms. She, as always, promptly calls back. I explain my symptoms. It feels like a success to say I have some frightening thoughts, BUT I honestly do not have a plan. I will not act on these intrusive thoughts: however, I don't feel the current medication dosage is sufficient. She agrees and makes some dosing tweaks. We will meet next week to evaluate the changes.

It hits me - how much easier the process is when I don't over-identify with these thoughts. It has taken me a while, but on certain days (like today), I can realize these are only signs of my bipolar. Not my identity. Not gospel truth. I am not a puppet controlled by a puppeteer of dark thoughts.

I perceive this incident as what it is - a physical manifestation of a chemical imbalance. Of course, my thoughts warrant immediate help, but the situation is much less stressful and frightening when thought of as purely a symptom of the disorder.

The symptoms remain severe but not all-powerful. They continue to impair but do not reign unchecked. I feel severe emotional pain, but because of my history, I know this too will wax and wane.

In the meantime, I must wait for the medication changes to take effect. I must do one of the hardest things of living with bipolar, sit in the discomfort. Acknowledge and be surrounded by pain without trying to escape. For now, just sit.

Delightfully Pink
July 2017

As I sit on the porch steps admiring this beautiful summer morning, there's no humidity yet. After a few days of rain, I'm in awe of the blue sky and green landscape. Cole is next to me, smashing, picking, and throwing petunias from my pot. He has far too much baby testosterone for simply smelling flowers. He pulls out a large fuchsia blossom.

I inform, "That's a pink flower. Mommy's favorite color - Pink."

The words have barely left my lips, and I realize what I've just said. For years I've been telling the kids my favorite color is gray. When you have kids, you get asked questions like this frequently.

Now there's nothing wrong with gray. It can be classy and sophisticated or a great neutral. But when I've told them gray, I've meant the stormy weather, blending in so as not to be noticed, hopeless gray. I didn't put conscious effort into finding one of the gloomiest colors to represent me; it just kind of happened. That's the color that screamed Leah and my identity. Gray has been my favorite color for years.

I try to think back to the last time my favorite color was pink. It was always pink as a little girl, even through my teens. When life, the depression, and the mood swings started getting harder than I knew how to handle, my favorite color changed.

It's not the color but what the color represents. To me, pink symbolizes cheer and spunk, femininity, and confidence. I am far from finished on this pink journey of walking confidently with my head held high and knowing my true worth, but I can feel something changing. I knew my original favorite color, pink, was back and that I'd made more progress than I had realized.

A Little Oomph
September 2017

There shouldn't be, but there is an overwhelming sense of disappointment. I've let myself down. After five years of managing bipolar outside of hospital walls, my mental state has become more than I can bear. My best bipolar management skills and impressive adherence to medication schedules aren't enough. The intrusive, suicidal thoughts consume every waking moment. I fight to keep it together, but I can't anymore.

However, something is different this time. I'm as depressed as I've been at previous points, but somehow a bit of hope lingers. I remember getting to this point in the past and still mustering up the courage to fight. Prior victories spur me on; they encourage me enough to not follow through with my suicidal plan.

I believe medications will eventually bring about change. I will begin to feel differently. But for now, the hope for change looks like hospitalization: hospitalization and waiting.

My movements are slow.

I cry continually.

I'm triaged and ultimately admitted to an adult floor for an undisclosed amount of time. As I start down the hallway, I observe the other patients and listen for clues about where I've landed. It turns out this unit is a bizarre combination of college students having their first mental breakdown and geriatric psychiatric patients trying to get medications perfected.

I follow the staff member to my room. It's always a gamble of who the roommate will be. This time it's one of the geriatric patients, Cynthia. Over time, I gather she has dementia and accidentally took the wrong medications. She is currently on "eyesight," twenty-four hours a day watch. Someone sits in our doorway all night long, technically watching only her, but it still feels intrusive.

After a few days, the psychiatrist determines Cynthia is safe enough to be off of eyesight; however, Cynthia is weak and struggles to get around. It isn't uncommon to wake up to, "Leah, Leah." Sure enough, the staff is gone, and Cynthia is stranded on the toilet again. She needs a little oomph, a one-two-three with an arm intertwined with hers, to get up. I awaken to her screaming my name from the bathroom multiple times a night. Out of fear of who could replace her, I don't complain. Truth be told, I also need a little oomph - an emotional oomph, so I am not one to judge.

I spend most of the day studying for missed graduate classes and attending the hospital's group sessions. I look forward to the daily fifteen minutes of sunshine in the courtyard. I get a few visits from family, but mostly I request they take care of the kids. I will be fine, but Tommy could use some help holding down the fort.

As the days pass, I develop a peace about being here. Something is different about this hospitalization. This admission doesn't feel like such a loss of identity. It's not an either/or; It's a both/and. I can maintain who I am while fully accepting the reality of being a patient. The hospitalization and medication management process seems so much easier when I give up resisting

I belong here for now but can also imagine a bright future outside these walls. Medications begin to take effect and make me feel more balanced, and the deathly whispers of depression have ceased. This change makes way for more hopeful thoughts. My plan no longer ends today. It's a longer-term plan - a plan for the future that involves picking up where I left off and finding the energy to continue the fight.

I have faith in the process, even when it feels like a setback.

Tux in a Prison
February 2018

It's been a couple of months since our well-loved dog Milo darted into the road, an intense season of mourning that non-animal lovers could never understand. Our elderly next-door neighbor dropped off cinnamon rolls. My brother and sister-in-law brought dinner. Another neighbor brought liquor. They are all animal lovers, and therefore they all understood that we lost a family member.

For weeks, I continually cry. My mind replays Milo's final breaths, taken in my arms.

As months pass. I'm finally able to think of Milo's life, the priceless memories contrasted by the horrific last moments, without crying.

I scour the Internet searching, 'When is the right time to get another dog?'

It appears that there isn't a set timeframe. Despite my hopes, the Internet produces no set waiting period. I'm left to decide for myself - left wondering if the time might be now.

I begin looking for a dog on a nationwide pet adoption site. There are thousands and thousands of available dogs. At first, I occasionally browse without any serious intent. However, with each search, the excitement wells up within my chest.

One by one, I read the stories of various dogs. Some are hopeful. Others are heartbreaking.

Following days of researching and attempting to find a match for our family, I come across Tux. He is a black lab mix that is approximately four years old. Tux's profile is brief, not overpromising, but it does indicate he is a good dog. His story is a bit unique. He was a stray. While at the shelter, a prison administrator saw Tux's sweet temperament and hand-picked him for enrollment in the prison's dog training program.

After a few phone calls, I learn more about the program and, ultimately, Tux. The administration has paired Tux with an inmate who trains him. They spend twenty-four hours a day together for three months, much of the time spent in a cell with a bit of recreational time in the yard.

The more people I talk to, the more I get the same vibe. There's just something extra special about this dog. Although many dogs pass through the prison program, this one is different.

Tommy and I decide to make the hike. We've got to meet this dog. Well, that's what I think. Tommy is more along the lines of 'We got a neurotic dog last time and what's to keep us from getting another?' But you know how it is - women just have this way of excitedly and continuously talking about an idea that there's really no way around it. So, yes, we drive a few hours to the prison.

We check-in at the front gate, give the guard our driver's licenses and go through a quick background check. Ultimately, we are allowed to enter, meeting with a supervisor and Tux. I see Tux's black body and white chest, hence his name. Sure enough, Tux is just as sweet in person as his description. He spends the majority of the visit resting on our feet. He doesn't jump. He doesn't lick. He doesn't bark.

The employee encourages me to see how well he does on a leash. I take the leash, and Tux nonchalantly comes along. The only dilemma is that there isn't much space to walk. We're in the entry room to the prison, and the only way to go is through the metal detector, so we go. Tux appears unfazed as we walk through with numerous beeps and alarms, likely due to the zipper on my jeans.

Within minutes, Tommy and I are both extremely impressed. Tommy is getting closer to admitting that I was right on this one. We agree to come back in two months when Tux will have completed the entire training program. We will be able to officially adopt him at that time.

How To Give an Unintelligible Speech
May 2018

Graduation from graduate school - I've never worked so hard for anything in my life. There have been more papers and presentations than I can count. Hundreds of clinical clock hours.

I have poured my everything into getting this degree on a daily basis for years and years. Abruptly, today, it is all coming to an end.

Other graduates, faculty, friends, and family fill the auditorium. I'm engulfed in emotions. For as long as I can remember, I've felt my feelings on a stronger scale than others around me. Today is no exception.

Initially, there is a sense of relief. I've finally jumped through enough hoops and strived to meet expectations for long enough. The powers that be are satisfied. I am proud of my accomplishments.

However, fear creeps in as I come face to face with the reality that I am about to be tested in the "real world." The swirling emotions lead to a weepy whirlwind, an eleven on a scale of one to ten.

After listening to a relatively typical send-off speech by the department chair, the class president moves to the center of the stage. With her peppy voice and bouncy curls, she informs us we will be doing superlatives, and each member of the graduating class is to give a short speech after receiving their award.

I internally panic! The center stage is not my comfort zone, so I cross my fingers and hope they forget me.

My stomach turns as I safely make it through eight classmates. "Most likely to bring cookies to class" and "Most likely to ask for an extension on an assignment."

Oh God, mine will be most likely to wear mom jeans or a frizzy, messy bun.

Then, I hear, "Leah."

As I rise out of my seat, "Your superlative is: Best Human. Mic Drop."

Oh wow. That can't be for me. So amazing but yet so undeserved. I have four steps down the auditorium aisle to compose myself and come up with a speech for that.

I (unsuccessfully) fight back the tears as I draw the microphone toward my mouth.

"What an honor, but I don't deserve this award.
If you only knew.
I have to thank God because there are so many reasons
I shouldn't have made it this far.
I had my son at sixteen.

I never imagined I would make it to college, definitely
not graduate school.
I can't take the credit.
I really want to thank God.
I also want to thank my friends and family for
supporting me every step of the way.
Thank you."

Tears continue to pour as I return to my seat.

I feel pretty confident that I didn't do terribly, considering
being put on the spot.

I squeeze in next to Tommy and whisper, "How'd I do?"

"Babe, I'm sure you did a really good job, but you were
crying so hard that no one could understand."

"Like not even a word?"

"Yeah, like not even a word."

Blubbering to the point of being unintelligible marks my
last moments at the University. In true Leah fashion, out with an
emotional bang. And a darn good speech, even if I was the only one
who could understand it.

Trouble at Sea
May 2018

Tommy and I bask in the summer sun, celebrating my graduation.
It's a strange but lovely feeling having the chance to enjoy the beach
alone - adults only. With the help of an arsenal of friends who've
agreed to watch the kids, we have five days to ourselves. We talk like

we did when we first started dating, without the feeling of being rushed. We still wake up at 6 a.m. because the routine of having kids screaming to get out of bed is just too deeply ingrained. We ride bikes down the sandy oceanfront sidewalks.

We even register for a dolphin cruise. I'm a bit skeptical, doubting we will see anything more than algae.

A jovial captain and the deckhand greet us. The boat fills as family after family piles on. At around twenty-five passengers, we are at capacity and head off. The deckhand spews facts about yachts in the marina and nearby beach-front mansions as we ride out to sea. We begin to pick up speed, enjoying the beautiful views as the shoreline fades into the distance.

Finally, after about thirty minutes, the captain reveals, "We are coming up on some dolphins. They are going to be on your right." Everyone looks and scoots to the right, as far as possible, without capsizing. Sure enough, there are dolphins, and they are beautiful! It is a mother with her baby that is only a few weeks old.

The boat turns in sync with the dolphins, keeping them in view. More dolphins are spotted. Announcements continue guiding us where to look. Another dolphin playfully jumps through the waves produced by the boat.

While in awe of the dolphins surrounding the boat, a blood-curdling scream pierces the silence, "He's having a seizure."

Tommy nudges me. "Babe, you need to go help." All of my inadequacies flash through my mind. I look around, hoping there is a medical professional on board. No.

I work my way to the inside deck. "I'm a retired nurse. Can I help with anything?"

221

I stare down at a small boy, convulsing with eyes rolling back in his tiny head. In a state of panic, his mother hands me her cell phone. I see the numbers 9 - 1 - 1 across the screen. The operator is already on the line.

I answer by saying, "I'm a retired nurse. I'm really rusty. Just tell me what to do and I'll do it."

The emergency operator states, "I'm just glad to have someone on the line who is calm. The captain is on another line and they are trying to intercept your boat, saving time from you all having to make it back to the marina. I'm trying to get information from his mom, but she is too frantic to answer. How old is the child?"

I act as a go-between. I must be calm if I'll ever be able to get any information.

I confidently, and as tenderly as possible, ask, "How old is your baby?"

She can barely speak. "Sixteen months."

With emergency personnel's guidance and a series of specific questions, we learn that the baby had a fever this morning, and the parents gave him medication that has likely worn off. Add the heat of the midday sun plus the additional warmth of a lifejacket; I can't help but assume it's all related.

I continue to relay information back and forth about his color, breathing, overall status, and actions to ensure his safety.

After six minutes of seizing, the child begins to whimper, a reassuring sound as he regains consciousness.

A few more minutes pass before we see rescue lights - paramedics arriving by boat. The parents transfer this precious little one, alert and crying, into the arms of the team which is prepared and waiting for him.

The rest of us continue our route back to the marina as planned.

As we return to our vacation rental, Tommy and I continue to think of that toddler and his family. I process by talking (and am sometimes guilty of ruminating). I can't help but discuss it with Tommy a few more times.

He praises me, "Leah, you did an amazing job with all of that. You were so calm and just handled everything. I could never do that. I just don't get it though. How can you handle something as terrible as a little kid having a seizure out at sea, but everyday things stress you out?"

I don't know.

Dr. Simmons would later explain the body's ability to compartmentalize stress during traumatic experiences. The task for me will be finding the triggers that lie within everyday life, the signals that often falsely indicate ordinary life is not safe.

The Gift of Music
June 2018

Over the years and following ECT treatments, I realize that music holds the key to unlocking memories that had once vanished. Music serves as a way to bypass the barriers of forgetfulness.

They say that music has the power to take us back in time. Certain songs have a way of reminding us exactly where we were when we heard them. It could be the first dance at a wedding. A song that played at a graduation ceremony. A "School House Rock" song from elementary school. The possibilities are endless.

As someone who struggles with memory loss, this musical superpower of songs means the world to me. There is nothing better than listening and thinking, *Oh my gracious, I remember this song, and I remember exactly where I was when I was rocking out to it.* The only tricky part is that I don't know which songs are linked with memories. Over the years, I've found a few.

My children and I enjoy listening to the record player in the living room. For kids who have spent most of their lives surrounded by modern technology, a record is a fascinating thing. One day, Mom surprises me with a gift - some old records that were tucked away at her place. I flip through and find "Puff the Magic Dragon." I place the record in the center of our record player, lower the needle, and begin to watch it spin.

As the music begins to play, a vivid memory suddenly washes over me. I am instantly reminded of sitting on my parents' bonus room floor. They, too, had a record player that I enjoyed as a child.

"Puff the magic dragon lived by the sea."

The music transports me to a time when life was joyful and carefree. I adore my parents, and they can do no wrong. I am young and singing along with no idea what the words may or may not have actually been about.

On another occasion, Boys II Men's "I'll Make Love to You" comes across my slow jam playlist. Within the first few seconds, I can picture myself swaying back and forth with my arms around one of my best friends at the 8th-grade dance. I made the wise decision to ditch the worthless guys I had briefly dated and go with a friend from the inclusion classroom.

I am wearing a light pink dress, not a pretty pink, but more mauve. The gown was recycled from some wedding I had previously been in.

My dear friend and purely platonic date is on the autism spectrum, so social events and close contact are a stretch. We do the awkward kid slow dance with my hands on his shoulders and his hands around my waist. We sway back and forth with our feet firmly planted. His anxiety manifests as rocking back and forth at least twice, maybe three times the speed of the music.

I vividly remember his words, "How did you learn to dance this good?" I chuckle.

A while later, I find another song with the ability to transcend ECT-related memory loss. I am a firm believer in listening to rap songs with a great beat while working out. Anything less would hinder the desired heart rate range and render the workout darn near worthless.

While huffing and puffing on the gym's stair machine, Tupac's "Changes" plays. I am immediately in a black Nissan Altima with pink fuzzy dice hanging from the rearview mirror and driving on the interstate to nursing school.

"That's just the way it is. Things will never be the same again."

These are the same lyrics that washed over my soul as my entire body was terrified to show up for another day of class and clinicals.

Some people appreciate music. I cherish and desperately crave the lost memories that music provides.

Music serves as a bearer of gifts. In these instances, the gift is of memories that I thought were gone.

Poster Child for Regained Success
July 2018

I've settled in quite nicely into a job. It is every new graduate's dream. I am a productive member of the workforce. This is the real world, and I am making it!

All seems to be going well. I provide the utmost quality of care. I socialize and build relationships with coworkers. I'm busy but happy, stretched but grateful. It's a great place to be.

I look forward to no longer needing disability as I'm finally able to provide for my family and myself.

It feels incredible.

Not So Fast
July 2018

It's a Tuesday morning and an hour into my workday. I abruptly start sweating. It's a strange sensation but nothing that can't be overlooked. A few minutes pass. My vision begins to tunnel until there's only a tiny field left. Still, I try to work while tilting my head and squinting.

Bewildered, I tell a couple of coworkers. They kindly urge me to leave work.

One employee reassures me, "It will be fine. We will take over everything for you."

I leave the office and head for a nearby urgent care. It's difficult to drive peering through a tiny field of vision, but I succeed.

Upon triage, my blood pressure is 158/100.

I've never had hypertension. That's when it hits me. *These are symptoms of a panic attack.*

This panic attack would be the first of many taking this form, with physical symptoms too intense to overlook. I begin having four to five panic attacks per week.

The struggles are not limited to work. I struggle at home as well.

Debilitating fear randomly takes over my mind and body. Everyday household events such as making dinner, taking a shower, or even just sitting on the sofa are not exempt.

Social anxiety increases as well. I become almost paralyzed in public. I humiliatingly shake and cry in stores. I tremor in restaurants.

My fantastic start out of the gate and into the real world has come to a screeching halt.

"Code Blue Adult"
August 2018

After a few months of being "normal," working fifty hours a week, attending to the kids, and running a home, I start a mental downward spiral. The desire to be normal is so strong that it overpowers recognition of the stress I'm under and the reality of my ever-present mental illness.

My mental state takes an even darker turn. Racing thoughts become increasingly filled with suicidal plots. Dr. Morris sends me to the hospital for evaluation, resulting in an inpatient admission.

My belongings are taken from me to be searched and held in a locker. Security wands me down with a hand-held metal detector.

I spend nearly twenty-four hours in a holding room while waiting for a room on the assigned adult floor. A psychiatric room can be hard to come by.

Once finally transferred from admissions to the adult floor, I'm given toiletries and towels and ushered to my room. My bag is held at the nurse's station, to be searched yet again. With no desire to socialize in the day room, I settle in my bed.

I am introduced to my roommate, Colleen. I can't help but notice her frail figure. She is unable to change her own clothes, so a staff member helps out. Once dressed and assisted to a standing position, Colleen slowly shuffles out of the room.

The hours pass by at a snail's pace. I don't care much for television, and my eyes (as a side effect of medications) are too blurry to read.

There isn't much to look forward to - just sleep and visitations.

Tommy comes to visit often. He appears to be handling this hospitalization much better than he could have handled even a small mood swing in the past. *Maybe we can make it. Perhaps I'm not too much to handle.*

Now, Tommy brings comfort instead of needing to be consoled.

I have other visitors as well. Camila and my parents come often. They smuggle in candy - my favorite.

I've become so sedated from the medications that I'm sleeping as many as sixteen hours per day.

In the middle of the night, my deep sleep is pierced by a loud thump and screaming. I immediately recognize the sound as Colleen falling. I yell through the dark, "Help! We need help!" Numerous staff members race through the door, working to get Colleen off of the floor.

From this point on, Colleen is kept in a recliner at the nurse's station. Each time I walk by, I can't help but notice that she appears to be getting weaker. I don't have a nursing license anymore, but I can still recognize that she is crashing.

I pray the nurses see what I am seeing. I doubt anyone would listen to me, a peon psychiatric patient, but it pains me to keep my mouth shut.

Patient, no longer the provider.

As the day goes on, I take another nap - one of many. However, I am abruptly woken from my slumber by an overhead announcement.

"Code Blue Adult, Code Blue Adult" called to this floor.

Oh God, no, please don't be Colleen. As I stick my head out of the door (against all the staffs' commands for the patients to get in their rooms), I see that it is indeed Colleen.

I lay in my bed, listening to each word that is said. My mind flashes back to the day when that was my job. I begin to shake, and an anxious feeling takes over my chest. The words *Code Blue, Code Blue* repeat in my head. I hear the psychiatric nurses fumbling through a medical situation until finally, the ICU nurses arrive from the main hospital.

I spend the rest of the day listening to another patient with dementia, Aleta, scream at the top of her lungs, "No, no, no, no, no!"

The combination of flashbacks to nursing days, *Code Blue* repeating in my mind, and Aleta's deafening screams are about all I can handle.

In an uncharacteristic fashion, but pushed to the limit, I storm down the hallways screaming, "This is not a therapeutic environment. Get me out of here. I want to leave. Get the doctor."

It is of no use. The staff at the front desk divulges that my doctor is not on call this weekend, and no other doctor will discharge me. I think it is a scheme to keep me here against my will.

In an attempt to pacify me, the nurse offers a quiet room and an "as needed" medication.

Xanax will have to do for now.

Chaplain
August 2018

A young man enters the day room with trendy, round glasses and patterned socks that peek through the small gap between the hem of his pants and dress shoes. He stands out from us - the bored patients of the psychiatric hospital. He is not one of the typical staff members either; I would know because I recognize just about everyone by now.

The new guy announces, "I'm the hospital chaplain. Is there anyone who would like to talk about something? Aaaanything?"

No other patients seem interested, so I take him up on the offer.

"I have a question, but it's a little deep. I'd rather not ask it in front of everyone."

The chaplain replies, "Sure, let's sit in those chairs at the end of the hallway. It's a little more quiet there."

I settle in the chair with skin adhering to the sticky vinyl material.

I explain, "I don't know why, but every time I think of God, I start to cry."

His face shows interest. "Hum, what was your experience of church when you were growing up?"

I tell of days in the youth group and how my father was an elder. "I think it was fine. This whole crying thing started later, like around the time life started getting really tough. It started around the time I was diagnosed with bipolar and everything fell apart."

Nodding his head and smiling a bit, he warned, "I'm a Buddhist, so take my Bible stories with a grain of salt."

I burst out laughing.

Then, the chaplain begins to tell of Jesus on the cross. "When Jesus was being crucified, he said, "My God, my God, why have you forsaken me?"

I wipe away a tear and ask, "Is that called a juxtaposition? Like when you know God is good, but it also seems as if He's forgotten you."

He agrees, "Yeah, yeah it is."

I reply, "I think you figured it out. I feel forgotten. But then it's reassuring to know I am not the first one to feel that way. Jesus felt that way, too."

We chat a while longer. I thank the chaplain for his time while he denies that he's done anything; just help me to find the answers that lie within.

This conversation would be the start of a new season - a season of no longer feeling forgotten. This realization marks the start of being able to think of God without crying as much. It seems so simple that acknowledging I feel forsaken would conjure up a mental counter-argument.

No, He hasn't forgotten me. No matter what I may briefly believe at the moment, it's not true. I am not forsaken.

{help needed}

Neurofeedback
August 2018

Camila is one of those brilliant friends who also keeps her opinions to herself. During today's hospital visit, I begin to pry.

"I give you full permission to speak freely. If I were your child, what would you do?"

Camila has seen all of my struggles with medications and side effects. She knows I'm refusing the doctors' latest plan, additional ECT treatments. She also knows of the dark places that haven't fully healed; the trauma that I try to act like doesn't bother me.

Camila sees through all of that, and she loves me anyway. For this reason (and the fact that she is a psychologist and knows more about the brain than just about anyone), I value her opinion.

It doesn't take long before she replies, "Leah, you have a very sensitive brain. I really think neurofeedback would be a good option."

At the next inpatient visit, Camila brings me a scholarly book discussing the success of neurofeedback used in the treatment of trauma.

I begin my research. I don't know if it will pan out, but it seems like a viable option to consider.

I would later travel eight hours to work with one of the most highly regarded specialists in this area of medicine to complete the intake process and brain testing. From there, I would undergo scheduled sessions at least three times per week.

However, as much as I would love to continue treatment, it will not be feasible due to logistics and time constraints. I mentally tuck this treatment away as a viable possibility for some time in the future.

Creepy Crawlies
August 2018

It's been years since I've had any visual hallucinations, but they've started creeping in again. Literally creeping in taking the form of spiders crawling on my chest and over my son's body.

Nightmares worsen, and I frequently wake in a panic. The same theme continues - being chased by rapists.

I share these disturbances with Dr. Morris.

She pauses for a moment, "These symptoms aren't coming from your bipolar. You need more counseling for PTSD."

I moan. I throw my head back and let out a frustrated, "Ugh."

"I thought I'd done enough work on trauma already."

She explains further, "Your mood is getting better but your brain is in a fragile state which is allowing the hallucinations to come through. The hallucinations are from PTSD."

It is tough to hear. It feels like such a huge setback - to instantly swap from thinking of myself as a strong survivor to plummeting back into the fragile victim role.

Longing to be healthy and willing to do whatever it takes, I reach out to the DBT therapist I'd seen in the past. She also holds special certifications related to sensorimotor therapy, often beneficial for individuals with a trauma history.

I sigh, coming to terms with my current, fragile mental state.

Here we go again. I wonder what treatment will entail this time. I wonder what the therapist will uncover.

I now understand why desperate individuals go to extremes looking for help. I am that desperate person. Nothing has worked for any significant amount of time. You name it; I'll try it. I'd probably even buy snake oil. I just want to be regulated and "normal."

Four-Legged Help
September 2018

My treatment team, family, and I have determined my symptoms are severe enough to warrant a service dog - another last-ditch effort.

Why not try to see if the dog we already have, sweet Tux from the prison, could work?

I decide to get him tested.

I miss sleep, wondering if Tux will make the cut. I watch every available documentary on service animals. Overcome with emotion, I end up weeping throughout these G-rated films.

I scour the internet for details about the differences in therapy and service dogs, possible tasks that a psychiatric service dog may perform, and the typical cost of training. I listen to podcasts and read books about the process of training a service dog.

I hope and pray that the local boarding school for service animals will see the same positive qualities in Tux that I do.

Debut in Training
October 2018

Just as I'd hoped, Tux passed the initial temperament test and is now participating in vigorous service dog training.

His vest is ready. I've excitedly covered it with patches in a collage-like fashion.

"Service Dog in Training."

"Not All Disabilities Are Visible."

"Please Don't Pet Me. I'm Working."

Tux and I prepare for our first public access debut. It's not as much about him. He is well trained, and I'm highly confident he will do wonderfully. It's about me. This outing is my debut.

As I gather my courage in the Walgreen's parking lot, I mentally question, *Do I actually want to walk through those doors with a service dog?*

Walking in with a service dog feels like a sort of coming out - a public display of what I've known to be true but have desperately tried to hide. If I have a service dog, the disability I have quietly lived with will be manifest for all to see.

In a split second, my thought process morphs.

I'm tired of trying so hard to hide my illness. I will benefit from a service dog, and I'm going through with this.

And I do.

As Tux performs wonderfully at Walgreen's and every subsequent store, my confidence grows.

He alerts me anytime my anxiety begins to creep up. He is trained to implement deep pressure if I have panic attacks in stores.

He ensures that crowds give me the space that I need. We make a fantastic duo.

It's a few weeks before anyone questions us (actually longer than I anticipated with all of the skepticism in today's culture).

As Tux and I are walking through the parking lot, a man who is sitting in his car rolls down his window and shouts across a few parking spaces, "Why do you have that dog? You don't look disabled."

I put on the most dramatic of responses, "Ah, that's highly offensive. He is my dog, and I do have a disability."

He appears repentant and seems to realize his mistake stating, "I'm so sorry. I mean you just look like a healthy young girl."

"That's okay. I get that a lot."

I smile and wave goodbye

Yes, that was an incredibly rude thing to say, but you know what, it also felt good to hear. For almost as long as I can remember, I've been trying to make sense of the fact that I do look like a healthy young individual, BUT I'm chronically and severely mentally ill.

That dichotomy is challenging to deal with, but today it all came together, visibly sorted out beyond the confines of my head, even if it was in the grocery store parking lot. And strangely, it felt validating to hear someone admit that I look healthy when I'm truly not.

The Planned Last Day
January 3, 2019

I am back at the very lowest of the lows. The downward spiral has rendered me utterly hopeless; at least, that is how I feel. The whispers of the past few months have turned into blaring screams, and there's simply no way to ignore them now.

Just give up. The challenges of life will never get better.

Depression has extinguished all hope for a better tomorrow.

I have just enough energy to comprise a plan - a dangerous place to be.

The medications, therapy, support system, service dog in training, etc., - none would prove to be stronger than my deadly thoughts.

My mind is a catastrophic whirlwind of ways I could kill myself; however, I go about the day in a usual fashion. The older boys catch the bus. I purposefully leave Tux at home. I take Cole to daycare.

In an eerie coincidence, he asks, "Are you coming back, Mom?" I lie through my teeth and promise, "Yes, Coley, I'll be back this afternoon."

I drive down the road to a grocery store, where I find a parking spot. I sit in the car. After nearly an hour of searching on my phone, researching over-the-counter medications that can cause fatal arrhythmias, I find what I am looking for. Multiple case studies confirm the deadly dose of a specific over the counter drug.

I march confidently into the store. To be sure, I buy what would be a year's supply of the medication. As I walk out of the building, I look into the "eyes" of the security camera and smile. This last footage should be accurate and representative of my true feelings - relieved and at peace.

It is time to bail. Today will be the end.

I drive to the most remote place I can recall. It's a thirty-minute drive to the shore of a deserted lake. I desperately want relief from the world's pain but would never want to inflict the agony of finding me upon a loved one.

I begin taking the pills, handful after handful. I finally get to a place where my stomach feels like it will explode. The back of my throat feels like pills are stuck.

I've ingested four times the lethal dose.

I recline the car seat, waiting patiently, looking forward to drifting off to sleep (eternally).

As I wait, my phone dies. It has a shortage issue that causes it to die for days at a time. It's okay as the dead phone is just one less way for anyone to find me.

About thirty minutes in, my level of consciousness begins to change. Something happens - something, unlike anything I have ever experienced.

Suddenly, I start seeing a mental video of my children, one by one. The center of the vision is clear, and the edges are slightly out of focus as if filmed with a fisheye lens.

It starts with my oldest, Jordan. It is footage of him grieving long after my death. He tries to remain strong and stoic to no avail. It quickly jumps to Micah. He, too, is grieving following my burial but differently and more visibly. And finally, the "movie" clips transition to Cole. His little mind is confused, repetitively asking where I am.

Then halfway between self-talk and an audible supernatural voice, I hear - "Leah, you f***ed up! You have GOT to get yourself out of this!"

I don't know if it was God. I don't know if God can say the F-word in emergencies, but it is at this moment that the gravity of my actions hits me.

I sit up and look around. There is no one in sight, so I grab my phone. Still shorted out and dead.

I cry out to the Lord, "God, if you let this phone work, I promise never to do this again."

The phone somehow powers up flawlessly with the push of a button. (A cell phone repair specialist would later tell me that there was no way my phone should have worked that day.)

I dial 9 - 1 - 1.

The operator answers, "911, What is your emergency?"

With speech beginning to slur, I utter, "I've made a huge mistake! I overdosed. I wanted to die. I've taken over two hundred pills."

"Was this intentional? "

I don't know how someone accidentally ingests a couple of hundred pills.

"Yes, I thought I wanted to die, but I now realize my kids will miss me. I need help. I'm so sorry that my mistake is falling on you."

Operator: "Just stay with me here. Can you tell me where you are?"

I reply, "I don't know. I just see ducks and a playground and a lake."

"Give me a second here. We are going to locate you. Help is on the way. I want you to stay on the phone with me until help arrives."

The operator's voice is comforting. We continue to talk for another ten minutes or so, until an ambulance and fire truck arrive.

I'm becoming more sedated. It is harder to focus.

With a bit of help, I wobble from my car to the back of the ambulance.

The crew seems relatively calm. The EMTs inventory the pill bottles, taking note of how many are missing. One man takes my vitals and gathers supplies for IV access. Another sticks EKG leads on my chest, and the spikes begin to cross the screen.

Upon looking at my EKG, the demeanor of the crew abruptly changes. One man bangs on the window to the front section of the ambulance where the driver sits.

I hear screaming, "We gotta go! We don't have time for a line (IV access)."

I am losing consciousness, and my EKG is morphing into a deadly rhythm.

I knew this would happen. I have to fight for my life.

One by one, my senses slip away. My field of vision darkens. My hearing is no more. All that is left is the sensation of the bumpy ambulance ride. But before long, that, too, fades.

That's all I remember... All I remember for the next few days.

I wake up in a hospital bed. I instantly pick up where I left off - fighting with every ounce of my being - fighting to make it.

As this point, fighting for my life looks more like fighting the staff as a severely confused and combative patient.

I am terrified. I realize what I have done but have no power to reverse it.

In a panic, I try to jump out of bed. Flailing and wrestling with the hospital staff, I mumble, "Am I okay? Is my heart messed up?" They sternly hold me down and insist I stay in bed.

Every time I attempt to get up, the staff reiterates the same script, "You are in ICU. You tried to kill yourself. You have to stay in bed."

A couple of minutes pass. Forgetting the rules, I fight to get out of bed again. Screaming for my glasses and wanting water for my severely dry mouth, and yelling to go pee despite a catheter.

Then, the psychosis sets in. Spiders are dropping from the ceiling and recoiling back up in a yo-yo-like fashion. The clock on the wall is morphing into a face coming toward me. The tile floor turns into rising, flooding waters.

The louder I scream, the more I get the same response. The sitter at the bedside reiterates, "You are in ICU. You tried to kill yourself. You have to stay in bed."

My family visits me in the ICU. I don't know how often or for how long; it is all a blur. They repeat how thankful they are that I survived.

I wasn't expected to make it. The immediate concern was the deadly arrhythmia. The second challenge would likely be severe brain damage.

After a couple of days, the psychosis resolves. There does not appear to be any brain damage.

I am stable enough to be transferred to the telemetry floor. I am improving, but my heart rhythm remains irregular. It will be nearly a week before my EKG will return to normal.

I am incredibly weak. It takes a two-person assist to transfer to the bedside commode, and I cannot ambulate without a walker.

I discover that a detective has impounded my car as evidence since I was expected to die shortly after the overdose.

From Medical to Psychiatric
January 2019

The week passes, and the medical doctor finally clears me. I earn a police escort to the psychiatric hospital.

I live in a relatively large city with numerous hospitals. Shockingly, this visit will be to a hospital I haven't been to yet - the fourth and final psychiatric hospital option in the area.

There are minor differences, but nothing drastic. I acclimate just fine.

From within the walls of the psychiatric ward and in between therapy sessions, I make calls to those close to me, apologizing for the pain I've caused. I telephone the police station in an attempt to get my car out of the impound lot.

And then, after a week in the psychiatric hospital with some minor medication tweaks, I am sent home.

Just a week?

To me, the psychiatric stay seems relatively short, considering the magnitude of the choices I have made and the near-death experience I just endured. I will have a lot of work to do with my outpatient therapist.

Enough Is Enough
February 2019

We, Tommy and I, have reached a point in the relationship that we cannot ignore any longer. The words that have been said can't be unsaid. Tommy doesn't forgive me for the suicide attempt. Even after attempted "make-ups," the tension is still palpable.

When weighing the option of splitting up, the decision becomes clear.

At this point, it isn't a blame game - it's a matter of what is healthiest for all involved. We mutually agree - ENOUGH. There are no winners or losers - just wounded individuals seeking a fresh start.

We put in our thirty-day notice to the landlord. Too broke to move out immediately, we rough it together for the final month. The first couple of weeks are filled with harsh words alternating with periods of poignant silent treatments (real mature, I know).

Then, the pendulum swings to some testing of boundaries and the search for any possible, lingering romantic feelings. Things fizzle out after a couple of rendezvous, ending in a rather peculiar but appreciated friendship.

This friendship would allow us to share in the excitement as the other would eventually begin dating again. Tommy would be the one to call on the third of January each year, the anniversary of my near-death suicide attempt. The calls are never filled with judgment or disgust but instead cheering me on for fighting another year, reminding me of my worth and future. Maybe more than anyone, he has had a front-row seat to the pain and madness. His kind words mean a lot.

Now, we don't co-parent flawlessly, but I must say we handle it better than expected. It's the trivial stuff that occasionally gets us. For example, in an attempt to foster independence, I have been known to allow Cole to dress himself and show up at his father's sans underwear and hobbling in snow boots in warm weather. Not quite Tommy's style, and I end up hearing about it later.

I am sure we will always have our differences, but I pray that we can always keep in mind what is best for Cole.

Tux and Taxes
March 2019

Tux is my sidekick, accompanying me to appointments and running errands. I never know when being in public will push me over the edge and trigger a full-blown panic attack.

But Tux knows.

This incredible dog continually monitors my breathing, knowing that a change in breathing equals a spike in anxiety. The trainers attempted to teach him to paw or nudge to alert for anxiety, but he wouldn't. Just when they feared he would never alert, Tux came up with his own mode of communication, a strong huff. It almost sounds as if he is sighing to tell me that I am sighing.

When I realized what he was doing, it was a relief. His sign is surprisingly more discreet than either of the other options, but it's noticeable to me. We have a secret code.

With a pat on his head and a "Thank You, Good Boy!", Tux has perfected his task of alerting me to my anxiety. By watching my breathing, he will even alert for suspenseful parts of movies I'm watching.

Tux also joins me at my parents' house. Today, it is time to work on taxes. Dad is great with numbers and helps me every year. I plop down in an office chair next to Dad. Tux, without being told, automatically does "under," positioning himself between the legs of my chair.

Dad pulls up the tax software on his computer and I type in the answers to the first few questions.

Then, that's where it gets a little more tricky. Dad steps in. He asks, "How much did you get in child support for Jordan last year."

Big sigh from Tux. I laugh. He notices my anxiety on that one. It's as if Tux can read my mind about the lack of child support - not nearly as much as was court ordered.

Dad, seemingly surprised, asks, "What was that?"

"That was Tux alerting for anxiety. He's good isn't he? Apparently he knows how little child support I got."

I realize that Dad hasn't seen Tux in action much. Of course, Dad has seen the vest and Tux following commands, but the alerting is more subtle.

Then Dad starts listening more closely. Sure enough, Tux alerts on a couple more anxiety-producing questions required to file my taxes.

But then, I yawn.

Dad, mistaking it for anxiety (now that we are watching it in an almost hypervigilant manner) asks, "What about that. Tux missed your anxiety."

I chuckle, "That wasn't anxious breathing. That was a yawn."

Dad questions, "He knows the difference?"

I chuckle, "Yes."

Dad and I play around. I try to fake a panic attack, even inserting a few yawns. Tux isn't falling for it.

Who would have thought that a dog could recognize my (genuine) anxiety? And even more impressive, notice it even when I don't see it coming.

Tux is a godsend.

I'd Never Wished for a Real Cockroach Until Now
June 2019

I sit on the outskirts of the playground doing the motherly duty of supervising Cole's play. I abruptly look down to see a giant cockroach run from my right shoulder across my chest. I panic, yanking my spaghetti strap shirt and almost, if not entirely, exposing myself. The bug vanishes as quickly as it appeared. I am left startled and hyperventilating.

Kelly, the forthright friend sitting next to me, fumbles for her words. "Um, Leah, I don't know how to tell you this. I know you saw it, but there was no bug."

The words sting, but I believe her. She has no reason to lie to me.

It is happening again. For once in my life, *I wish the cockroach were real.*

I go about the rest of my day - cooking, cleaning, and playing with the kids. Kelly and I even take the kids downtown to Monster Jam. It's a blast. We are home by midnight, but I can't sleep. Looking back, I realize it's been a few days without sleep.

At 2:30 a.m., I find myself crawling on my hands and knees around the bathroom floor. More bugs. I get close and try to crush them. I get right on top of them and lunge, but the toilet paper I'm using to squish always turns up clean. No bug residue whatsoever.

The squishing turns to sobbing. *These bugs aren't real either.*

I am beginning to feel strange sensations all over my body. It feels like itching and crawling. I am constantly scratching and slapping these palpable, tactile hallucinations.

The following day, at my request, my parents drive me to the psychiatric hospital. This admission marks my first hospitalization for manic symptoms, days without sleep, and tactile and visual hallucinations. I've had smaller issues in the past, but this is hallucinations on steroids. I cannot manage this on my own.

{doctors and fairy godmothers}

Off-Label Borrowing
June 2019

I have had so many failed attempts at striving for normalcy. Past hospitalizations seem nothing more than a band-aid, a temporary patch. I am uncertain of what novel revelations can come out of this hospitalization. Good God, please, something.

From the start, this admission is different. This hospitalization is the first time I can have Tux with me. He has completed all of his training and the necessary documented hours in public. Tux has transitioned from "in training" to "fully certified."

Accompanying me during this hospitalization requires more skill than one might imagine. He is on duty most of the day, unlike the previous outing here or there. Tux must acclimate to the staff taking him out to use the restroom and eating and drinking at the nurses' station.

This first night, I continue with the trend of not sleeping. Tux stays in the room with me as I pace back and forth. He snuggles with me as I stare at the ceiling for the remainder of the night.

Morning comes and after zero sleep, I enter a consultation room with a doctor I've never met before. I am still swatting at tactile hallucinations. My speech is faster than usual. My body aches, but I wouldn't consider myself tired.

I look at the doctor's badge, "Chief Medical Officer." He explains that he has touched base with my primary psychiatrist, Dr. Morris. Together they have reviewed all of the medications I have tried - every single FDA-approved medication for bipolar. Despite various medication combinations and strengths, bipolar continues to triumph. The drugs have not proven enough to curtail my dysregulation.

Dr. Morris has always had a sneaking suspicion that I have some type of genetic abnormality. The side effects of medications are just too prevalent. Sure enough, the results of some tests are in - and indeed, I have a genetic abnormality that causes poor metabolism of the medicines. *Go figure.* But somehow, this anomaly still offers a new glimmer of hope.

Now, the doctor overseeing my care while in the hospital comes up with a new plan. Borrow a medication from another class. The psychiatrist prescribes a drug that is typically reserved for schizophrenia. It can have some nasty side effects on the immune system, so I will require frequent lab work.

I don't care what it is or what it is for; just let it work.

Within hours of taking the first dose, I am overwhelmed by the most incredible sedation I have ever experienced in my life. And this is just the starting dose. I will need to continue increasing the daily dosage to reach a therapeutic level.

Loyal Tux lies with me.

The staff wakes me occasionally, including for our morning paperwork. I remember very little of what I write. I do, however, remember the question, "How do you feel?"

My reply: "Damn near comatose."

With that clarified, I go back to sleep for a few more days.

When I finally emerge from my hospital room, I am encouraged. I feel more mentally regulated than I can remember. *This is good.*

Tux continues to do well. He joins me during groups and waits outside the curtain as I shower. He does his command, "down stay" at my cafeteria chair as I go through the lunch line, flawlessly waiting for me and saving my seat at the table.

Tux reaches near celebrity status in the hospital. His nails clicking on the tile floors announce his coming. His friendly, furry demeanor brings a smile to just about everyone. He even rolls belly up and takes a nap on the floor during a group session providing comic relief.

After a few more days of medication titration, I have reached a therapeutic level.

I am discharged to follow up with Dr. Morris. As required, I will go to the lab every week for blood work and monitoring.

But there is a small glitch. Dr. Morris (and many psychiatrists) do not have the specific training required to legally dispense this medication. I fear losing her in exchange for finding a doctor to prescribe this medication that I so desperately need. I think the world of Dr. Morris and have been with her for years. She graciously completes the required courses to obtain her certification - to be my prescriber and to keep me as a patient.

I cry with gratitude for her dedication to my journey.

―――――――

It won't be easy, but this medication will prove to work in a way that nothing else has. After a decade of experimenting with various medication combinations and begging God for stability, who knew relief would come from a couple of round, white pills?

Life Within
Present

Once the depression and instability subside (not entirely, just enough), my purpose and passions are now center stage, ready to play their parts.

I have broken out of crisis mode and into the phase of creating a pleasurable existence. It is mind-boggling to transition from survival mode to genuinely thriving.

It is truly a blessing to be present in this life. My days start with a smile. But let me clarify, it's a small smile. I don't do big smiles or laughing until around noon. I still function under a medication-induced fog in the early hours as my nighttime medications have yet to wear off.

Take it from Micah. Within the first week of summer vacation, he said, "You are way happier when you don't have to wake up early." Sleep schedules and grogginess remain a constant battle, but not as bad as they have been.

Some days, I wake up at the same time as the kids. On other days, I sleep quite a bit longer. I am thankful to have reached a stage where Cole can be awake unattended without being a safety risk. I know what he does when he is up by himself. Try to hack the password on my phone to play games. Turn on the TV and watch a hefty amount of cartoons. He also makes himself breakfast, which typically consists of an ungodly amount of goldfish crackers and a few granola bars. Whatever it takes. I'm just thankful for the extra sleep.

On the kids' school days, when extra sleep isn't an option, I struggle a little more. I've been known to set multiple alarms and drink a hefty amount of caffeine.

On good days, I stay awake and get things done. Sometimes, I return to bed for a few more hours. Either way, I try to not be too hard on myself - to not compare myself to productive friends who can function on five hours of sleep. For me, it is typically ten to twelve hours, but it doesn't matter. It is a trade-off that I must accept if I'd like stability in the remaining, awake hours.

I can now exercise consistently. I take out the frustrations of the day on the treadmill and weights. When the gym is empty, which it often is, I enjoy dancing to my playlist between intervals. I've recently taken up boxing, not to fight someone, but for the stress relief and confidence.

There are still days when I don't feel like doing anything. I lie on the sofa binge watching series. After each episode, I attempt to mentally hype myself up to get moving. On my most sluggish days, physical activity looks like walking Tux around the block once, and that's it.

I'm reminded of something Dr. Simmons told me years ago, "When there is wind in your sails, that's when you go." This provides a calming bypass of the thoughts that say I should be more and do more. When there is no wind, I rest. When there is wind, I trudge forward.

I still ferociously contend for my health. I have monthly labs and relatively frequent appointments with Dr. Morris. Sometimes, my medications stay the same for months, but at other times, dosages require frequent tweaking. A little less of this, or a little more of that.

I've learned to have patience with the process. Medication side effects are just expected. This leads to a little less frustration and disappointment while I attempt to trust the process.

At my latest appointment with Dr. Morris, I update her regarding my situation. "I feel "normal," and I wish I could stay like this."

Dr. Morris honestly responds, "You won't stay like this but I'm glad your mind has gotten used to this period of stability."

I appreciate her candid response. Dr. Morris is right. Fleeting normalcy is destiny for someone with severe and persistent mental illness.

I am still missing plenty of memories (even years). I guess it is fair to say that if it hasn't come back by now, it probably won't. I try to spend less time focusing on what I don't have and instead, looking forward to a bright future that I will be able to remember. I am grateful for what I can learn and retain. I still do a lot of Google searches for things I used to know, and that's okay.

It is difficult to navigate severe mood swings while trying to earn an income – to provide for my family with the intent to get off of disability. I currently work as a health coach, helping others navigate and achieve their wellness-related goals. I can't think of anything I'd rather be doing.

Working for myself allows me to arrange my schedule around my children's needs and my inevitable bad days. I genuinely believe that my struggles with anorexia, numerous psychology classes, and remnants of nursing school knowledge all help me to succeed in this business. It's the thing I've always hoped for... using my struggles to help others.

Personally, I still wrestle with self-image and how to nourish my own body. I look in the mirror, and my eyes immediately scan toward the areas I don't like, noticing areas of pudge and perceiving chubby areas as more prominent than they are. Perhaps these critical thoughts will last a lifetime.

However, I treat my body with care – something I have not always done. I feed it regularly and recite words of affirmation. I've realized that eating a tub of ice cream or a box of donuts can't get me out of a depressed episode, even when my mind whispers that it will. I've noticed correlations between eating better and feeling better. I think about all my body has been through over the years, and I'm just thankful to be in this healthy state.

Socially, now that outings are not so frightening and anxiety-provoking, I can say "yes" to more. I went to a concert at a beautiful venue with stained glass windows and a huge crowd. That would have never been an option a few years ago.

I am able to schedule activities weeks in advance. Before, this wasn't possible as I didn't know what state I would be in tomorrow, let alone next week. Of course, I still cancel occasionally, but not nearly as much. Now, my calendar is filled with fun events – kayaking, white water rafting, walking with friends, coffee dates, and evenings around my firepit. I treasure these moments with friends and family.

As my social tolerance has increased, I have developed a love for thrifting. I'm not bothered by the odd smell of thrift stores; the one shoppers can't quite pin down, possibly mildew and grandparents. The hidden treasures take priority. There is a thrill in finding clothing for my children and decorations for the house. Friends and family will occasionally send me a wish list. If I can't find it at a thrift store, no one can.

I have taken up hobbies that I'd never considered while hospitalizations and sedation consumed my life. A hopeful life looks like caring for indoor plants that I'd never been able to manage in the past. I went from one plant to two plants to twenty. It is rewarding to keep something alive and watch it flourish. The greenery symbolizes the life and growth that I now treasure.

The kids and I recently rescued two kittens. I'm not really a "cat person." Tux will always have my heart, but the cats' spunk and passion for fun are wearing off on me. We laugh at their crazy antics at least ten times per day. Everything is a toy. Even poor Tux's tail is fair game.

I've been in a healthy relationship with an incredible guy for over a year. He understands my struggles and supports me; however, he does not try to micromanage my symptoms or medication changes, leaving that up to my psychiatrist. He cherishes me and treats me like a queen, something I thought I'd never find. As a single parent himself, he sees my children for what they are - a huge (although occasionally difficult) blessing, but certainly not baggage.

Will the relationship last? I don't know, but the casual nature of the relationship is perfect for right now.

Notice I didn't put the romantic interest at the top of the list? It's not because he isn't incredible, because he is. It's because I've learned who I am, separate from a relationship, and that has been an incredibly rewarding process. I enjoy the company but don't "need" him. This freedom, stemming from self-confidence, personal experiences, and blossoming hope, is liberating.

Life Surrounding

There are certain moments when it hits me how fortunate I am to be alive.

Jordan will be graduating high school in five weeks. Tears well up as I consider that I almost missed this monumental event and didn't realize he would still need me.

A few months ago, I had the strangest experience. I couldn't sleep, which because of my hefty night medications never happens, and I felt the urge to pray for Jordan's safety. I found myself praying to the same God that I've struggled to trust.

The following afternoon, Jordan called me completely distraught on the way home from school. While on the interstate, a full sheet of plywood flew into the front of the car. The debris was lying on the highway and was picked up by the tires of the large truck in front of him, thus rocketing the wood into Jordan's vehicle.

Jordan was able to safely make it off the interstate. The 4x8 sheet of wood took out the front bumper, radiator, and engine. There were no fluids left, and the collision shop could read the letters on the plywood still wedged in the engine. The car was totaled, but Jordan was untouched.

The next day, I shared about the incident with our neighbor, a police officer. I don't know if he likes my dramatic stories, but I figured he would find this one interesting.

The officer said, "Oh, I know about the plywood on the interstate. I worked the case with the same plywood, at the same spot, just yesterday. But it went through the guy's windshield."

I'm shocked. I hesitantly ask, "Did he make it?"

"Nope, it decapitated him."

I fight back the tears and think back to my sleepless night of prayer. Thoughts race. *Oh my gosh. That poor guy who didn't make it! But Jordan, what if I wasn't around to pray? What if I didn't believe enough to pray?*

I am beginning to trust. I am beginning to trust my intuition, God, and the process.

Then, there is Micah. He shared how kids were bullying him at school, saying, "Nobody likes you. Go kill yourself." He almost didn't have me available to help him and raise hell on his behalf.

Around the time of puberty, I was present to hear Micah's deep voice turn into another voice I know all too well - depression. Micah admits, "I have frequent thoughts that wish I was never born." Tears well up inside of me. I beg that the Lord would spare him from the painful path I've endured. I will always support him as we fight for the best treatment for his struggles.

And little Cole, I was blessed enough to watch him experience the wonders of the beach for the first time. We held hands and jumped over countless waves. I wouldn't trade that precious moment for the world.

It was an honor to be present for Cole's first season of basketball, games filled with traveling and the referee tying shoes. Cole is so used to playing ball with his older brothers, an adult ball, and a 10-foot goal that it took him most of the season to stop drastically overshooting. As a suicide survivor, I was just so thankful to be alive and cheering.

For the longest, I thought that I was only around for my children. Of course, they are a highly motivating inspiration. But they are not the only reason to keep fighting. I never considered the positive impact I could have on the people in my circle and those I meet.

I am reaching a level of stability that allows me to evolve from self-preservation to emotional presence for others. I was walking in the neighborhood when my fifteen-year-old neighbor ran up to tell me that his father had a massive heart attack in front of him and ultimately died. It was an honor being there for him and listening as he processed and shared the heartbreaking details of what he witnessed.

I was around to watch a friend's daughter so that she could go to a job interview. She got the job, which made a substantial financial impact on their family.

It has been an honor to donate to a fund for a three-digit crisis line, ultimately working towards suicide prevention.

I have been blessed to partner with organizations that provide housing and education for young men in Uganda and clean drinking water in Kenya.

It is also with gratitude that I'm able to donate food to the same charity that once provided meals for my family, a full-circle opportunity that "privileged" hardly begins to describe.

I was alive and present to take a dear friend's phone call when she was suffering from postpartum depression and having frightening thoughts of hurting herself and her children. Without her knowledge of my personal experiences, I don't know that she would have felt comfortable enough to share her struggles, let alone heed my recommendation to contact the doctor immediately.

It is the highest honor to be considered a safe place for others.

I've learned to sit with individuals who are going through various hardships without feeling the need to fix anything - just to be near.

I've learned to ask specific questions to friends and loved ones who are down.

"Can I ask you something, because I love you dearly? Are you suicidal? Do you have a plan? Can I sit with you while you call for help?"

My darkest experiences are not without purpose, and neither are yours.

Conclusion

I am thankful to be here to write a conclusion, but not just any conclusion - a conclusion that does not conclude. This tale does not have a magical storybook ending. I didn't pray my mental illness away, and I haven't found a phenomenal, permanent fix. And I certainly never found "normal."

Instead, the future chapters, yet to be written, will inevitably be engulfed in uncertainty and varying degrees of illness. But, they will be written.

At this point, it has been two years since my last hospitalization - really good for me. Dr. Morris categorizes my mood swings as "subclinical," meaning my symptoms no longer dominate my everyday life. I am grateful. My friends and family see it. I feel it. My Dad describes this current version of me as "different as night and day."

I can't believe it has been this long, over a decade since these struggles began. It would be a complete lie to say that the blows of life have gotten any easier, but my mindset has changed. I no longer look for reasons to "justify an out" or wait for a time to quit.

As Dr. Morris says, "Life has gotten so much easier since you decided you don't want to die."

No matter how hard, I don't want to miss a thing.

Out of The Mouths of Babes - Happily Ever After

Cole, now five years old, was on the playground with a much younger friend. Suddenly, Cole for seemingly no reason announced, "My parents are split up. My Mom left my Dad, and then, happily ever after happened."

In many ways, I feel like this IS my happily ever after. Just the fact that there is an "after" is happy. I live each day with gratitude, knowing that previous suicide attempts could have prematurely closed my final chapter.

I still have occasional panic attacks and depression continues to make daily life a challenge. I stress about bills, struggle with self-doubt, fear my parenting isn't good enough.

BUT I have realized how thankful I am for every day, even the ridiculously tough days.

Now, as far as Cole's perception is concerned, I am not sure if my life meets the qualifications of a kid's version of "happily ever after." I don't play all day, my fairy godmother hasn't whisked away the trials and tribulations of life, and I still take naps, but I'm thankful he sees me as happy.

I may fly under the radar as relatively stable for a while, possibly even years at a time, but eventually and inevitably, my symptoms will rear their ugly heads. However, I am much more regulated now.

I also know now that, regardless of what highs and lows are yet to come, none of them will be worth permanently quitting over. I have a counter-argument to that horrific little voice that says, "The world would be better off without you."

Leah, even at your darkest, weakest moments, you are not a burden. Quitting life is a burden. The world is ALWAYS better with you.

Dear One, this goes for you as well. You are not a burden. The world is ALWAYS better off with you!

As I continue with introspective work, I look back over all the energy I exerted to appear "normal." It all seems in vain now. Who cares about chasing "normal"? It's an illusion, like a mirage in the desert, with no award at the end. The endless chore of pursuing "normal" is an isolating demon.

There is no "normal."

Instead, how about we fight for hope? We hold onto any glimmer, no matter how tiny it may seem. When hope is in the ring with despair, despair may seem louder and stronger, especially after days, months, or years of misery. Hope's voice may become drowned out and hard to hear. But it is unwavering. It is always there whispering, "You matter. You have a purpose. Someone smiles because of you."

With each beat of your heart and every breath, hope triumphs.

Listen to the still, small voice.

It's not a false illusion - it's the strength that carries us through.

While writing this book, I have tragically lost three more people in my circle to suicide. The pain and sting are incomparable and absolutely gut-wrenching.

We have lost another one of "us."

What can we do? How can we prevent the toxic and deadly whispers of depression?

I wish I had a magical solution, but I hope that sharing my story opens honest conversations and decreases the stigma associated with mental illness.

I'm telling you (as I hope you'd say to me), we will continue the fight. Hold onto whatever minuscule amount of hope you can grab. Hold it tight, and don't let it go. Hope is the key.

With hope, we persevere.
With hope, we live a little lighter.
With hope, a tiny glimmer of light pierces the darkness.
With hope, we don't have to try to get back what was lost.
With hope, we anticipate the blessings yet to come.

With hope, we realize this season is temporary.

With hope, the waves of pain don't crash down quite as hard.

With hope, we have a future.

With hope, we realize our stories don't end here.

With hope, we know there are beautiful chapters yet to be written.

With hope, anything is possible.

Hold onto hope, Dear One.

Made in the USA
Middletown, DE
14 January 2023

21539688R00166